C000067986

STOCK MARKET OPERATORS

INVESTMENT GREATS

STOCK MARKET OPERATORS

By
George F. Redmond

Introduced and Edited by
Donald Mack

PEARSON EDUCATION LIMITED

Head Office:
Edinburgh Gate
Harlow CM20 2JE
Tel: +44 (0)1279 623623
Fax: +44 (0)1279 431059

London Office:
128 Long Acre, London WC2E 9AN
Tel: +44 (0)171 447 2000
Fax: +44 (0)171 240 5771

First published in the United States of America in 1924

First published in Great Britain 1999

© Pearson Education Limited 1999

ISBN 0 273 64311 8

British Library Cataloguing in Publication Data
A CIP catalogue record for this book can be obtained
from the British Library.

1 3 5 7 9 10 8 6 4 2

Typeset by M Rules.
Printed and bound in Great Britain by
Biddles Ltd, Guildford & King's Lynn

*The Publishers' policy is to use paper manufactured
from sustainable forests.*

ABOUT THE AUTHOR

George F. Redmond

In keeping with the limited printing facilities inherent in book production in the early part of this century, most authors seem to have kept personal details about themselves to a minimum. Looking at this book by George Redmond we are hard put to find out very much about the man himself. He writes very lucidly about the lives and accomplishments of the great American market operators, financiers, and industrialists of the past 50 years looking back from 1924, but of himself we learn very little. He obviously enjoyed finding out what characteristics had shown themselves to enlighten us on what made each of these personalities the success they were. Initially he wrote up each individual's personal sketch for a magazine article and they were later separately published as such. Obviously realizing that he had assembled more than enough material for several compendiums of the wealthy and the successful, that certainly led him to the medium of the published book. No television back then, it was definitely the printed word that carried the day – newspapers, magazines, and books of every description, all of which were favored by him. Besides this book *Stock Market Operators*, written in 1924, he also has to his credit *Financial Giants of America*, an earlier work in two volumes with sketches of the leading well-known financiers and industrialists in the United States during the 1880s to the 1920s.

ABOUT THE SERIES EDITOR

Donald Mack

Collectors in their particular field of personal interest always seem to start with a few things that intrigue them, then as the years go by their collections, like Topsy, just grow and grow. Well, that's what happened to the editor of this classic book series. At first he acquired several books on the stock market. Then a collection started and it grew into some 200-plus books. Finally, it came down to gathering one copy of every book ever published on markets and on investment and trading. Before it ended, the collection was easily some 5,500-plus market books and a lot of bookshelves.

It all began when he bought a few New York Stock Exchange shares in his youthful exhuberance, and wow! the profits just rolled in on those first few transactions (something not unusual for first-time investors to experience on their initial market forays). Then buying and selling more, he quickly discovered he wasn't quite the natural market genius that initial results had given him. Then from beyond the blue came that still, small voice whispering "Hey kiddo, if you're going to be serious about this trading and investing, you better do some studying (actually one heck of a lot more studying) or you ain't going nowhere."

So it was that he went from introductory general investment books to detailed general investment books to Fundamental Analysis books, and lastly to Technical Analysis books where he found a lifetime of study. Meanwhile the books continued piling up and piling up more and more. The answer – his Investment Centre Bookstore in the late 1970s and through the 1980s in Los Angeles, the only one in the USA that specialized in stock market and commodity books, both new and old. He discovered the greatest Technical Analysis books of all time were written 30 to 60 years ago, and the big surprise – they were just as good today and just as applicable as the day they were written. Since markets basically don't change (one buys on them, one sells on them, and prices are recorded with every transaction), price action charts don't change (prices go up, they go down, they go sideways), and investors and traders don't change either (they keep making the *same* mistakes since Adam and Eve first invested in Forbidden Fruit Inc.).

While he always stocked the bookstore with the market books in print at the time (ho-hum), it was those superb old market classics ranging all the way from the great general ones to the great technical ones of decades gone by that had his interest. Definitely *not every* book published during those decades was a great one, but Madame Greatness produced more than her fair share. The net result of his exposure to so many classic market books over the years, was that he gained an appreciation and a fair amount (and a bit more) of knowledge and expertise on these books. Then came a meeting of minds with our good publishers, the Financial Times Prentice Hall of London, England who saw the potential response there would be in bringing back from obscurity all the great classics that this editor suggested.

Working together, the American editor and the British publisher have inaugurated a marvelous series of great Technical Analysis classics which is still growing with new additions. For investors and traders far and wide they can now invest in the growing, not-yet-finished *Traders' Masterclass* series of classics which is now joined with this second now underway series named the *Investment Greats* series. The first series is the cream-of-cream in Technical Analysis writings; the second series ranges from classics, strong with technical content, all the way to no technical content at all. Every book will be found to be a gem in its own right and in the special investment area it covers. What a collection both series will eventually make together!

CONTENTS

THE INVESTMENT GREATS SERIES

What type of investor are you? Do you make choices or follow rules? The greatest investors have always combined a strong awareness of guiding principles with a breadth of market vision that separates them from their peers. For the greats, schooled wisdom is elevated by instinctive imagination. Flair like this does not come easily, but through immersion in the inspiration of others, it can be encouraged and developed.

Selected and edited by experienced US trader and renowned investment book expert, Donald Mack, the *Investment Greats* series offers a glimpse into the psychology of the world's great investment minds, bringing together some of the classic investment literature of the past 100 years in a newly presented, modern format. For years these books have been hidden from all except a select few, but once again their secrets can be appreciated and absorbed by all. The *Investment Greats* series demonstrates the enduring power and quality of investment art.

This series will benefit and inspire investors at all levels with provocative ideas and timeless wisdom. It provides tools and techniques, but most of all, it offers a reader-friendly, literary style and a passion for investment which is as refreshing as it is infectious. These are unique classics with a personal voice.

If you appreciate the art of investment, the *Investment Greats* series will take you into the minds of the masters.

EDITOR'S INTRODUCTION

It has been said that "History is bunk," but we who pursue learning about stock and commodity markets find that the history of these markets and the people who trade on them can only be ignored at a peril to our bank accounts. For there really is no way that the persevering market student should be unaware of many of the historical individuals and personalities each decade who rise to stratospheric heights and fame for their outstanding trading and/or investing abilities. And, if proof were needed, then this book is the acme of a collection of market minds and personalities that taken *en masse* could easily be said to have set the standard for the "Golden Age of Market Operators and Personalities." While the book takes in a wider range of time (about 50 years) than might be expected, there is an advantage here that is extremely fortunate for us in that its author, writing in 1924, was close to and possessed so much firsthand knowledge of so many of his subjects. Today we would be hard put to find any group from any period in American history that could be said to be anywhere near the equivalent in stature of those whose sketches appear in this book. Also here we have the benefit of history hard at work, making it possible for future generations to have the passage of time to prove or disprove any errors or contentions that might arise.

While delving into the personalities who have been included in this book, any financial market historian worth his salt would have to say "Wow." For, as said above, *en masse* especially, their likes in the challenging markets of speculation have not been seen since they made their marks either side of a century ago. For this statement to be really exemplified, all we have to do is to turn to the first chapter of the book. Here the place of honor to be the first written about goes to probably the greatest American speculative trader of all time – James Robert Keene. Now on hearing that name it would not be the least bit abnormal for practically every reader to comment on and question this description by asking "*Who* did you say?" Then this will almost surely be followed by the similar sentiment that "He can't have been all that good for I certainly have never heard of James Keene who was probably the greatest American trader of all time."

Well, that would be the response from practically all market people everywhere, with very few exceptions. For if we were to ask, say, 10,000,000 or more investors across the United States today who was the greatest trader ever, or who was James Keene, it is safe to say that only a handful would know the correct answer. The reason for this particular lack of knowledge is not at all hard to work out. All roads generally point to the villain in the piece and this leads most times to just one factor, the greatest enemy of good books and interesting people – the passage of time. Old man "fickle time" has it in his power to pick and choose who stays known and who is forgotten. So it seems that time made its choice in Keene's case. The decision – obliterate another of those who lit up the speculative heavens in their allotted Earth time. If anyone can be chosen to head the list of those time has obliterated, Keene has to be the prime candidate for he truly shone with as bright a brightness as trading markets have seen. However, like all the shooting stars that pass Earth's way, they come, they shine, they illuminate their particular milieu, then the same light just fades away – and so many times that is it!

However, it doesn't always have to be so, especially these days with the all-pervasive media having both the resources and the . capability to draw attention to, or against, practically anything they have a mind to. That same media attention can work very positively if it so chooses, where we find a part of it working, in this case, for the restoration of almost forgotten classic market literature – reversing time's earlier, now temporary, obliteration. This book by George Redmond and the others in this Classic Series have been turned into an overwhelming example of this restorative power, enabling students of speculative markets to now survey that which time had previously denied them. By bringing back truly great market books, such as this one by George Redmond with its 1999 re-publication, Financial Times Prentice Hall of London, England, makes its mark in this specialty area. For with this innovative push to revitalize the market book classics, with this particular book for example, some famous and some deservedly, but not so famous, market personages have the unique chance to receive their due recognition again.

Especially so should that be the case for James Robert Keene, otherwise known as "The Silver Fox." Hardly ever has a star of such speculative stature and proportions gone so unnoticed by later investment peoples, but that is exactly what has happened. As you will read further on, he came as an 18-year-old to the United States in the latter half of the nineteenth century, from what could be described as Dickensian-style London, England. Certainly not the background we would expect to see for one who was to become America's greatest trader. And just how did this come about? Well, for a start we do not want to give away that which the reader will soon discover in the following pages for him or herself; however, it certainly is a fascinating story.

It's also one that richly deserves to be passed on to all who belong now or will in future times belong to that widespread community of speculative traders and investors who really should, and hopefully will, appreciate and develop the knowledge and sense of feel for what has gone before. They who forego gaining an intimate grasp of prior markets and of the people who made up those markets can still progress notwithstanding that they choose to ignore the past. However, this disdain has ways of getting its own back in future trading and/or investing, for just as ignorance of the law is no excuse, ignorance of past market history and movement will often result in detrimental effects to one's profit/loss accounts. The gods of the marketplace do not take kindly to those who fail to grasp that nothing happens in isolation where markets are concerned.

Falling closely on the heels of "The Silver Fox" came one of immense trading stature, one who time was to prove possessed all it took to be one of the very few who was recognizably positioned to challenge Keene's "greatness" credentials. For here was an individual who very early in his own lifespan saw his market activities earn for him the title that was never to be lost – "The Boy Plunger." Starting at the youthful age of fourteen and showing a natural Mozartian-type analytical trading ability of immense proportions, Jesse Lauriston Livermore was, with Keene, the brightest of the bright stars in those same heavens of market speculation. However, where Keene has remained the unknown of unknowns, it has been just the opposite for Jesse. For, unlike practically all the great names that have found their way into this extremely rare book, that was not what fate had in mind for Jesse, and to this day he remains so well known that we can say he has been immortalized. In his own era, even without the advantage of today's mighty media and communications networks that can cover the Earth in a matter of seconds, he easily made it to the top of the media of his day. With a lifestyle that was as flamboyant as his fame, and a gift for the spectacular, it all suited him very nicely indeed.

If Jesse's trading activities and personal renown had been subject to the treatment rendered by time's usual destructive power in the way just about all the others in this book have been, his fame and much of his story would still be there to enthrall the future generations of investors. For into that fabled life in the very early 1920s (we do not know exactly when or how) came one possessing a power of his own – the ability to write and to write well. So it was that Jesse Lauriston Livermore met Edwin Lefevre and Edwin met Jesse, the combination which was to immortalize Jesse probably forever more. It certainly had to have been unforeseen then, but out of this partnership in 1923 came the most popular market book ever to grace bookshelves anywhere – *Reminiscences of a Stock Operator*. A book that year in and year out through numerous printed editions starting with the very rare 1923 First Edition has sold and sold and sold. There is no stopping it and probably a hundred years from now it will still be the inspiring bestseller it has been the past three-quarters of century from the time it first saw the light of day.

Considering all the market books that have been printed since 1923, one could reasonably have expected *Reminiscences'* light to have been overwhelmed by scores and scores of later masterpieces, but it hasn't happened yet, and I for one certainly would bet that it never will. Ah, but many would say, surely markets have changed tremendously since 1923 and Livermore's operator times. The answer would definitely be in the affirmative. Present-day markets have to be described as being very, very modern. In matching our very progressive times, they have been electronized, mathematized, computerized (and all other "izes"), leaving them far different from those of years ago.

In that light today they might say that Jesse Livermore would just be another institutional trader or one of the boys on the floor. But the truth inherent in all free speculative markets is all to the contrary. Taking a knowledgeable and realistic view here, not only are today's speculative markets *not* even one tiny iota different from those of times that have preceded them, they will *not ever* be any different from those that follow at any time in the future also. For all free speculative markets have exactly the same *raison d'être*, the same reason to exist as they have before now, have now, or will ever have. External and internal market conditions and mechanisms are unarguably constantly changing. There is no question that a great many changes have taken place and will take place. This can be seen in the growing numbers of shares, futures, derivatives, bonds, etc. that are exchange handled; in the interplay of different world markets in the amounts and types of paper exchanged; and in many ways too numerous to mention.

But still it should not be hard to recognize or accept that markets always have and always will perform *just one basic* function. They had the same function in the very first speculative European markets in the seventeenth century, they also *solely* have the same function today, and they will have the same function in the foreseeable (and even the unforeseeable) future. That function comes down to two separate, but really identical actions – someone physically buys something at the time (in our current usage this being some speculative piece of paper or electronic equivalent), and at the same time someone sells it to them or vice versa. *Any market* anyone cares to mention anywhere will see a market that absolutely *does not care* and really does not give a whit for the milliard reasons the sellers are selling or the buyers are buying, nor whatever paper or electronic equivalent is being exchanged. Every single one of these markets in itself just does not care in the least who is doing what or why: the "who and the why" just don't mean a thing. Financial markets are there for buying something and equally there for selling that something, with the additional task of factually recording and reporting each and every transaction. That is their total essence and again that is entirely what they are about. Everything else is periphery and does not come into the two basic market functions which are the *only* thing markets care about – the act of buying and the act of selling on those markets. Whatever the reasons for these actions, they remain the sole property of each buyer and seller and that is where they totally remain as far as each market is concerned.

So despite the many basically superficial reasons many well-meaning investment people attempt to make for their case that markets are different today than, say, in Jesse Livermore's time (or any time before or since), they are not. If Jesse were to return to the markets of today, he would almost undoubtedly, after some familiarization, be able to pick up where he left off earlier and still be as fine an operator as he ever was. The thing that should be noted here was that *Reminiscences* was published in 1923 and this particular book by Mr Redmond in 1924. There was no way that this author could have had any idea that his book, containing material about a contemporary of his, could possibly foresee that Jesse was also in the process of being immortalized.

This alone illustrates the one great advantage that this Redmond work possesses. In 1924, he was either very close to, or not too far removed in time from, every single person included in his coverage of great market operators. This closeness is as important to us today as it could be, since writers in our time wishing to examine the same lives, such as those men Mr Redmond chose to write about, have to base their material on the results of their own scholarly research. Today's writers totally have to depend on what they would be able to garner from books, from records of these men of times gone by, and possibly from someone still around at the time who was knowledgeable about the subject being written up. All of this has to be tempered with the fact, and it is a fact, that historical inaccuracies are the order of the day time after time, and then many times they are unknowingly perpetuated as fact years later. Not so for the subjects of these sketches of Mr Redmond's, these great market operators were of his time and his witness is of those times and moreover of his own personal knowledge of most of those he wrote about. We are the richer for this fact for we are hearing from one who was there, not a secondhand account passed on with vital details sometimes missing or possibly either lost or misunderstood.

Thus do we see this great advantage displayed many times in a number of the sketches in the book. This really is exemplified in his chapter on Jesse Livermore where things we knew, and especially other things that we didn't, are passed on to us firsthand and give us the feeling that we are hearing them from a close acquaintance who really knows the person he is writing about. And then there are other things, which add to our knowledge on each subject that, because of the book's extreme rarity, have escaped the attention of later writers on the same subject. Yes, we really are the richer for this knowledge which some 75 years later is again available to us. With the re-publication of this long-lost book, this unique collection of men who made their mark in their own times now gain a new appreciation for their contributions to our common heritage. As a sidelight to the many women who read this book, in the reference in the text to "this unique collection of men." Wall Street really was a male domain back then. If the author had so chosen he could well have added the one very, very notable female market operator of those same times – Hetty Green, "The Witch of Wall Street." But he didn't for reasons we know not, so we'll just let it go and leave it at that.

The third very memorable character in this book (especially to those well versed in the knowledge of his financial pursuits) is Jay Gould, the railroad magnate and superb market player. In his period of being on the public stage, like Jesse Livermore, he was the media darling of his times (the "Number One" so it would appear), but "darling" might be, and really is, too extreme a word when applied to Jay Gould. For example, in a typical utterance about this man and his lifetime activities, it was said by one of his contemporaries: "His touch is the kiss of death." Added to this was a slight touch of anti-Semitism, for with a Jewish sounding name he was sometimes accused of so being, but this was not so. With the media unanimously against him the whole of his business life from 1865 to 1892, he came to be known as "the most hated man in America" for many real and imagined reasons. Probably more the latter than the former. However, looking at and operating in the real world, most times one isn't accomplishing all that much unless one raises some hackles along the way, and Jay Gould definitely had a special talent for and an incomparable expertise in raising hackles.

Though some compelling reasons could be made for the attitude of the majority towards this unique character, the man's hard-nosed market and industrial successes at a time that America was experiencing tremendous expansion in its industrial growth leave little basis for the over-displayed hatred. On the surface it can appear to be justified for he did carry ruthlessness to its highest extreme. However, with Mr Redmond having the comparative luxury of time's passage and more factual records to make a fairer appraisal, he surmounts the earlier prejudices. In doing so he sets the record more in line with the man's great accomplishments, accomplishments that more than erase his personal deficiencies. His contributions to the expansion of American industry, and along with that same expansion its stock and commodities markets, has to forever enshrine him in its glory. Even the re-publication of this notable work on market operators will perhaps add to that glory, for now a wider audience will come to be much more familiar with Jay Gould and his greater plusses than minuses.

The fourth of the more famous great market operators to be covered in the individual chapters that follow, as in the mold of *all* those covered in this book, was a "one-off" and in his own way a mighty spectacular one too. However, his life story, unlike the more distant names covered in some other chapters, was one of immense fame and one garnered from his many roles in American life. His name, Bernard Mannes Baruch, or Bernie Baruch as he was and is so widely known and even more respected. His inclusion in this particular work might at first seem strange to the bulk of the American public, especially to those not aware of his earlier years. For the reality is that it was his later-in-life deeds that really made his name, and much, much less his earlier achievements that gained him his deserved entry in this book and to the levels of the highest order of America's greatest market speculators and operators. But there is no mistake here, Baruch earned his laurels for his legendary market activities at the turn of the twentieth century when he was just in his twenties and thirties. But legends on their own do not always stand the test of time. So it was with millions who had or have only a limited knowledge of the stature of the man, and it has to be said that his market life lies almost totally forgotten today.

However, when it came to his public life, this was a powerful testimony to his deeds that far outdistanced his earlier, forgotten market fame. At the time Mr Redmond was writing this book there was no way that he could have known the real fame that was to fall on Baruch's shoulders though he certainly had suspicions this might be what the future had in store. For probably in the entire history of the United States of America, no other single person, it would appear, has ever exerted their influence on American life more than he did. In a period spanning some 45 years (after his active market operations had ceased) he was known as the confidante of Presidents, every single one of them who served in that high office during and after his World War I years, and regardless of their Party. It has also to be noted that except for one stint of public service that occurred at the time of that war when he was appointed the Chairman of the War Industries Board under President Woodrow Wilson, he never held any public office, elected or appointed. Yet, his fame endures to this day as the unofficial presidential advisor over the many years of his long life. His office was a park bench near the White House where he could usually be found at times during the day, earning him the not-to-be-forgotten title, "The Park Bench Statesman."

Just as Baruch was certainly one of the great and recognized names in American life in the first half of the twentieth century, he was also well acquainted with another equally famous name during his market days, one which should endure for a long, long time. It was not just for his sumptuous lifestyle that many in his time took offense at and frowned upon (equally so that of his close friend and a market operator, "Diamond Jim" Brady). No, John W. Gates will always be associated with *that* name – "Bet-a-Million" Gates. Not to be downplayed, but at a time when a million dollars was more like a hundred million dollars in our time it counted a whole lot more, comparatively speaking. John Gates earned every penny of that name, for in reality he was always prepared to do what his name said. Such was his style that he was known to bet that amount on which of two raindrops on the window of his private railway car would hit the bottom edge first. In an age of flamboyance centered on the 1890s and the 1900s, "Bet-a-Million" stood out like a shining beacon.

But in life when the pendulum swings one way, it also swings back the other way, so "Bet-a-Million" was not without his own particular brand of opposition. We must, however, give him his just dues. Not for him was the opposition at all to come from the more populous heavyweight division of the then American financial world. No, for him, as it turned out, his had to be the Super-Super Financial Heavyweight Champion of the World who was to dog him here and to dog him there. But to also give Gates his added just dues, he wasn't the least put out, so it appeared, and he was equally capable of doing a whole lot of dogging back. This naturally begs the question just who was this "major force" who was dedicated to stymieing him whenever he could? Well, it was none other than the most powerful monetary force in the United States at that time, and equivalently at any time in our history. It can easily be said this individual, the likes of whom we have not seen again and probably will never again see, was that banker extraordinaire and lender of last resort to the US government when it had a great need for extra funds – J. Pierpont Morgan.

To J. Pierpont, Gates appears to have been too ostentatious, too brash, and too crude; still he was such an important force in the American industrial arena, J. P. had to deal with the man, mostly at a distance when possible. But after some titanic battles between these two in the 1890s and at the turn of the century, it was J. P. Morgan's turn to slightly prostrate himself (certainly a gigantic step for a man who must have hardly known the meaning of "slightly") before John Gates. The year was 1901 and Morgan had the vision to gather as much of the American steel-producing industry that he could into one major company to be called the United States Steel Corporation. Starting with the primary acquisition of Andrew Carnegie's holdings for $350,000,000, the largest in the industry and the key to the US Steel formation, who else after Carnegie should be next in importance in steel making and steel products? None other than "Bet-a-Million." Savoring his position Gates played it to the hilt, and should have changed his name to "Bet-a Lot-of-Millions" for that is what his steel holdings were worth and that was what Morgan, in effect, had to pay him. But Morgan was not really concerned about any of the amounts he laid out, for when shares in US Steel were sold to the public in 1901 (and over-subscribed too), he was left with the controlling interest at no cost to himself in this the largest ever US corporation up to that time. The amount J. P. initially paid out was totally recouped, plus there was an extra $25,000,000 that came his way from all the dealings. Nice work if you can get it. J. Pierpont Morgan was no slouch when it came to "getting it" in banking matters.

He was also no slouch when it came to the making of a market for the shares in the new corporation, for he knew it would be of vital importance to keep up the value of the new corporation on its introduction and that it would take someone with a particular talent to control the buying and selling of the shares on the New York Stock Exchange. For this he obviously wanted the best and the best is what he got, none other than our now old friend from Chapter One, James Robert Keene. The Silver Fox lived up to his name and reputation here doing such an exemplary job managing this debut of a major company's initial offering that it has historically ranked as the greatest introduction of its type in a major market that has ever been seen.

However, as this comprehensive work covers many other market operators besides those already mentioned, the author (and we too) can look at several in this book that J. Pierpont could also have selected for this vital market task. The competition was not minuscule by any means even if those same names remain almost unknown and forgotten today. First there was Thomas W. Lawson, another of the number of market operators whose name in his own time was known from one end of the United States to the other. For Lawson the act of *not* being secretive about his very successful market operations and activities was something against the nature of practically every other operator around. But, that wasn't the way Thomas Lawson operated. He had to broadcast it to one and all, and this in the light that he just pre-dated that new development – the "radio" – which in his time was just around the corner. Proving the pen is mightier than the proverbial sword, his finest writings and bestseller status came on the heels of his great 1905 book *Frenzied Finance: The Crime of Amalgamated*. This great work shook the foundations of Wall Street, but it didn't break them, and the outside public for once really got an extremely close (and not very pleasant) look at what happens at times behind industrial and financial doors.

Then there was Roswell P. Flower – plain ol' farmer's lad Roswell Flower in the last third of the nineteenth century. Livermoreian flamboyance was not at all what Roswell was about, but when it came to putting it all together in the stock market of his time, he was a "Wheaties Champion of Champions", a persistent bull on the American industrial scene and, strangely for an intense market operator, very much on the political scene too. A true "diamond in the rough" for plain ol' Roswell, whose appearance and speech hid some great talents, was also a former Governor of the great State of New York, a former member of the House of Representatives, and a possible nominee for the office of

President. As the author points out, the truly great market operators come in all sizes, shapes, and spectrum thinking. Each mold is individualistic and succeeding operators over the years have not in the least strayed from this lack of pattern. Taking them separately, or even in a group, there appears no rhyme or reason as to whom the market gods in their great wisdom choose to be members of that extremely exclusive club.

Two others of the greatest of market operators whose names deserve to be enshrined in any "Market Operators Hall of Fame" (should there ever be one) would be two, again, totally "unknowns" – Addison Cammack and Charles Woerishoffer. In their time, cherished names in the Wall Street firmament, and again deservedly so. They were good and really good at what they did, which was to speculate in stocks and commodities and only for their own accounts too. Besides Cammack and Woerishoffer, there are other unknowns, or almost unknowns, we also can enjoy meeting in this book on the best of the best of market operators, names that should not be omitted from honored mention here. Names like Thomas F. Ryan (the "F." standing for "Fortune"); Henry H. Rogers (the mighty power alongside Rockefeller in Standard Oil); "Uncle Russell" Sage (the creator of US market options among other things); William B. Thompson (a mining market operator without peer in mining shares); "Deacon" Stephen V. White (not really a "Deacon", but a man of unusual courage who turned a mighty fall into an even mightier come-back); F. Augustus Heinze (a great market operator, but one who never made it back after taking the fall), and Allan A. Ryan (son of Thomas F. and an exception to the rule that great operators' sons never even come close to matching their fathers' deeds), going on to be the architect of one of the greatest "corners" in Wall Street history – that of the Stutz Automobile Co.

As you the reader move from this Introduction to come in contact with probably the finest collection of operating market minds in the history of American speculative markets, the feeling to be gained here is "inspiration" from the strengths of these characters who have gone before us and have set the example. Some of you reading this after 1999 when this book was republished are going to be, or will be striving to be, successor market operators directly in the overall mold of these "greats." They weren't perfect specimens of human beings (none of us are), they may not have always operated according to the book (if there is such a thing), but they were giants certainly worthy of emulation in general and also in particular. So go and be likewise, they have pointed the way!

DONALD MACK

Series Editor
E-mail: Dmack144@aol.com

FOREWORD TO FIRST EDITION

From personal contact with thousands of investors and traders, covering a number of years, I am forced to the conclusion that there is a popular misconception of the stock market operator – his methods of operation, his purpose, his function with respect to the securities market and his status in the financial community.

Men like Keene, Rogers, Gates, Flower, Baruch and Livermore, all representative types and much discussed operators, at times have been condemned for contributing nothing to the financial structure of the country.

Sensational and uninformed writers with slight background of financial experience have fostered the illusion that the market operator is the serpent in a financial Eden. By misinterpretation of facts, causes of normal swings of the market have been distorted into machinations of a Machiavellian mind, when, in fact, the operator merely analyzed fundamental conditions more shrewdly and was thus quicker to foresee price changes.

Activity is a prerequisite of public interest in the securities market. It is the one greatest means of focussing attention and crystallizing opinion. An inactive security is never a popular one. If it has been the function of the stock market operator to create activity, it has usually been with the purpose of focussing attention on some particular issue.

While delving into the fascinating life stories of some of Wall

Street's famous men, I gained a passing impression of the market operators, which led me to further study of their activities.

It became increasingly evident to me that, contrary to general opinion, they represent real, vital and constructive forces in the financial world. Even more, a study of their operations brought out the fact that they contribute to the market many things that are of inestimable value to every investor.

Many do not know that without "Jim" Keene, the stock of United States Steel Corporation, today one of the standard investments of the country, might have lain dormant, almost unknown. It was the great financier, Morgan, whose genius brought the corporation into being, but it was Keene who, in creating the market for the stock, made thousands of permanent investors in Steel, stabilized the market and thus centralized the funds that have enabled the vast Steel Corporation to become the industrial giant it is today.

Without Russell Sage and Jay Gould, rapid transit in the city of New York might have been delayed for years. Without Colonel Thompson, investment partnership in the porphyry coppers, which revolutionized the industry and has given America world supremacy in the red metal, might never have been possible. The great resources of the South might have remained untouched for many years, but for John W. Gates and his coterie of financiers.

In merchandising, no matter what or how good a manufacturer's product may be, it will remain unsold unless popularized. The same is true of many securities.

My conclusion, therefore, is that the stock market operators are the greatest popularizers of securities. They perform through their market activities, the same functions as the widely distributed newspaper advertisements, albeit in a more effective way.

My admiration for their individual and collective achievements is profound. In the men I have studied, I found a combination of high courage, keen and penetrating vision, daring, fearlessness, and above all, the spirit of venture. These are men who stake their all, win or lose, modest in victory and grinning in defeat.

Not all of them have been successful, as these sketches will disclose – if success be merely the accumulation of personal fortune.

But they have played a great part in promoting the true function of the securities markets – that of creating public interest in stocks, through which the lifestream of industry flows.

As in my previous collection of sketches, *Financial Giants of America*, I make no claim to literary style, or to originality of material. My effort has been to gather much information that has hitherto been fragmentary, and present it in compact form, with the idea of enabling the reader to obtain a clearer perspective of these "plumed knights of the financial arena."

George F. Redmond.

Note: These sketches originally appeared in a weekly publication between August 11 and November 24, 1922.

JAMES R. KEENE

Keene was probably the greatest single power in the arena of the New York Stock Exchange. With his name is coupled practically every major market movement in the score of years preceding World War I.

To him was entrusted millions of dollars. His fame as a stock market operator of high courage, daring, adroitness and success will live in the financial history of the United States as one of its brightest pages.

JAMES R. KEENE

In the great arena of Wall Street, no man ever demonstrated a greater mastery of tactics and strategy, a broader outlook, or a more balanced judgment than James R. Keene.

Professional stock market operator, juggler of millions, contemporary of the ablest financiers of one of the greatest eras of American financial history, Keene directed some of the most spectacular market movements that ever took place in the world's largest security market. To Keene, as absolute dictator, was entrusted the resources of the biggest banking houses in the world. In his market operations he was, literally, the master of millions of dollars.

The part played by the professional stock market operator is little known to the public, just as one sees, in war, the fighting man, but suspects little of the master strategist back of the lines, directing the attacks and retreats.

Is the control of a desirable railroad available in the open market? The man who wants to get it, and get it at a fair price, calls to his aid a tactician of the caliber of Keene.

Is a group of bears, whose profits are made out of short selling and endeavoring to force down prices, to be severely punished, or caught in a trap? A market operator of Keene's type sets, baits, and springs the trap, without the bears even suspecting it until fairly caught and squealing.

Or is the stock of a young corporation to be protected and a fair market made of the issue, instead of being stifled to death by a group of destructionists? Let the professional operator of the ingenuity and adroitness of Keene stand guard.

It was to "Jim" Keene that J. P. Morgan turned.

It was in this latter connection that Keene reached the height of his fame. To him was entrusted the beginning of the market career of America's first billion dollar company – the United States Steel Corporation.

It was to "Jim" Keene that J. P. Morgan, Sr. turned when the giant combination of steel properties was completed, to see that a fair and equitable market was established on the New York Stock Exchange. Morgan knew that it was a gigantic task. The announcement of the formation of the corporation was sufficient to make the wolves sit up and lick their chops. And Morgan knew that unless he took extraordinary measures, he was merely preparing the feast.

To James R. Keene, veteran of a score or more of titanic market operations, was entrusted the spending of the Morgan millions to insure fair play for the stock of the United States Steel Corporation. And Keene conducted that market to a success that will long be remembered in the history of Wall Street. Because the public found a broad and active market in which they could buy and sell securities, they became investors in the stock. And subsequent quotations and dividends tell how well those investments turned out.

Keene's entrance into the stock market of New York City forms an interesting phase of his career. We first hear of him in San

Francisco. Keene, however, was an Englishman. He was born in London in 1832. His father, of North Ireland ancestry, was a small merchant, and young Keene was educated in a private school in Lincolnshire, later going to Dublin. The family came to America in 1850 and settled in San Francisco. Keene did all sorts of things after his arrival in this country, even to caring for horses and teaching school.

It was shortly afterward that the whole country was electrified with the discovery and opening up of the Comstock lode in Virginia City, and to this scene of turbulence Keene was attracted. Here he developed the latent sense of speculation that subsequently dominated his whole career. In Virginia City he accumulated a small fortune, sufficient, in fact, to return to San Francisco where it is evident that other things began to attract him. He bought the *San Francisco Examiner* and edited it. In the meantime he studied and practiced law for two years. All this, of course, broadened his viewpoint, and while the speculative fever abated to some extent, it was, nevertheless, destined to be the dominant force in Keene's career. It was but natural, with his success in speculation in Virginia City, that he should be attracted to the San Francisco mining exchange, and it was here that Keene began the development of that success in matching wits that made him the greatest market operator of his period.

Keene's career, however, must not be imagined as a series of continued successes. Shortly after he began operating on the San Francisco Exchange, an unexpected movement in the market of the Comstock issues found Keene on the wrong side of the market and he went broke. He was, however, not to stay down long, and two years later we find him back in the market again. But in the interim he had built up a reputation for sagacity as an operator that attracted the attention of the whole financial community in *Keene's market* San Francisco. Among the men who *successes have never* were impressed by Keene's ability and *been equalled.* judgment was Cornelius N. Felton, who was then one of the most powerful operators of the Pacific Coast, and when Felton became Assistant Treasurer of the United States, he sold his seat to Keene.

Keene, who then revealed himself as the most skillful and masterly member of the whole organization, was made its president. In the meantime the market movements of Comstock securities were becoming more violent. Keene, trading in thousands of shares, built up his fortune of some $3,000,000.

They used to say in San Francisco, and probably still say today, that Keene's market successes have never been equalled. His contemporaries then, as they were in his later life and operations, were the biggest men in the field. Among them may be mentioned names built into the romance of the Pacific Coast, such as Flood, Fair, Mackay, O'Brien, Mills, Ralston, and Baldwin.

In 1877 Keene thought he needed a vacation and decided to visit Europe but got no farther than New York. The New York Stock Exchange began to fascinate him and so great was its power of attraction that Keene postponed his visit to Europe indefinitely. Here began the career that was to make him pre-eminent in the history of American finance.

Keene's early operations on the New York Stock Exchange soon convinced him that operating on the Pacific Coast and operating on the Atlantic Coast were horses of different tints. Keene was accustomed to play the game by putting all the weapons on the table. But he soon found out that in New York the methods of those days were to put the gun on the table and keep a knife up the sleeve. He decided, therefore, to play a lone hand. He was not looking for help and to the end of his career he never asked for assistance. He was always the man who was sent for in cases of financial emergencies. Keene landed in New York with about $4,000,000, which was chipped away somewhat in his early operations. His courage and daring in the market attracted the attention of Jay Gould, but Keene decided, after several joint operations with Gould, that he would be better off operating alone.

The real beginnings of Keene's fortune were made in a period similar to that which existed in America in 1921. The panic of 1873 had left in its wake discouragement, not only throughout the business of the country, but in Wall Street. Keene saw that the country was recovering but that Wall Street was still in the "gloom" stage. Prices of securities were pretty close to the levels at which the panic had left them and Keene started to buy to the extent of his entire resources.

It was just the thing the market needed. That little stimulation was the touch that set the bull market on its career, a bull market which lasted through 1879 and 1880. Keene made millions and his original three or four millions were doubled and trebled. Incidentally, Keene had made a big reputation for himself. He was acclaimed one of the most brilliant and daring stock market operators the Street had, to that time, ever encountered.

There is no doubt that Keene took tremendous pride in his success. Like Alexander, he began looking for more worlds to conquer. He spread out into everything. He even tried to sit on that pinnacle from which so many have fallen – a corner in wheat – and as "pride goeth before a fall," so the inevitable happened: Keene went broke. It was his second failure and his last.

The tale of his rehabilitation is obscure, but subsequently to 1884 Keene was involved in the largest financial operations in the country and we find him aligned with such men as J. P. Morgan, *It was Keene's brains backed by Morgan's money.* John W. ("Bet-a-Million") Gates and the Standard Oil crowd. Keene is credited with having conducted successful market operations in Sugar, National Cordage, Third Avenue, Brooklyn Rapid Transit, Tobacco, Metropolitan Street Railway, Hocking Coal & Iron, and many others.

Probably one of his greatest achievements was his successful market operations in Sugar stocks, in which securities Keene literally created a roaring market over a period of two years from 1895 to 1897. In 1901 we find him conducting the memorable operations in United States Steel, and in 1905 the central figure of the market in the famous Amalgamated Copper. In the famous Northern Pacific "corner," when Harriman and Hill-Morgan forces locked horns for control of the Northern Pacific Railroad, it was Keene who was sent for by the Hill-Morgan interests to get every share of stock that was available on the Exchange. The shares were then selling around $100. Keene got them, and incidentally a price of $1000 a share was made for Northern Pacific stock, but it was Keene's brains backed by Morgan's money that made the coup successful.

"Jim" Keene had many friends – and (what successful man hasn't?) many enemies. He was a menace to the overambitious promoter, who attempted to dispense his wares at prices that were *No one ever knew* outrageously high. He was likewise the *what Keene was doing.* friend of many corporations that needed help in establishing public confidence in their securities when they were selling too low. But he was square. His word was sacred. He never gave a promise, but it was scrupulously fulfilled.

Some of the old-timers in Wall Street, chiefly those who crossed swords with Keene, and were beaten, will say he was ruthless, cold-hearted and iconoclastic. But there is more to his credit as a constructionist than there is on the reverse of the medal.

But no one ever knew what Keene was doing. It was impossible, so great were his operations, to tell whether he was buying or selling. He left no tracks, he had no confidants. But every time there was an important market move the word went around that Keene was in it. At one time nearly every tip that was circulated in the Street had the tag that "Keene is buying."

He was merciless to those who refused to play fair with him. The story is told that a group of financial interests approached him with a view toward establishing a market in a new industrial security. Keene made them agree to deliver all the stock they owned to him. His operations reached far beyond the expectations of the crowd, and they endeavored to beat Keene to the barrier by selling large blocks of the stock short. Keene saw through the trick, and forced the price of the stock higher. Then he called for delivery, and made the group cover at the top prices. Then he smashed the price, by throwing huge blocks of stock into the market, and when the smoke had blown away, Keene had the spoils and the would-be financiers had a working knowledge of Jim Keene's code of ethics.

One of Keene's chief characteristics was his directness. There were no long-winded conversations, no "beating about the bush." Either things were or they were not. He never wasted time or words. He never temporized. He would or he wouldn't. It was "yes" or "no." He would see you if you had something worth while, and cut right down to the heart of your proposition.

His office was one of Spartan simplicity. The windows were screened halfway up. This was to keep out prying eyes. Keene's visitors were big men, and the mere fact they were seen in Keene's office would have been sufficient to set the Street by the ears. For the Street could create in its own mind what such a visit meant, and get ahead of Keene. An able and efficient secretary guarded the door.

If you got in you saw a nervous, active man, with white mustache and beard, a pair of deep-set eyes, probably moving up and down the room like a panther, except when the ticker began to talk about the price of the stock in which Keene was operating. Then he became immobile, especially when things were not going just right. He heard what you had to say, and answered you, curtly, but positively. And when he was through, you realized that you were dismissed. He had no time for small things.

It was time for action.

And when Keene went into action, he swept the whole Street along with him. His brokers were innumerable. Fifty might be acting for Keene, and half of them never suspect it. They might buy and sell, but they never knew what Keene was doing. There was only one man in the world who knew that – James R. Keene.

There was another thing that only James R. Keene knew – the extent of his benevolences. There are today many men in Wall Street that can attribute their success to some kindly act of Keene's. As illustrative of this side of his character the following story is told.

In the old mining days, when the real struggle was on, Keene had many friends. One day he heard that one of the old-timers of the San Francisco days was "up against it." The man was then old, and his prospects were black for the evening of his life.

Keene, it is said, went to see him, and pulling a sheaf of securities out of his pocket, created in the old man's mind the impression that he and Keene had made the investment in those securities jointly several years ago, and he was, therefore, entitled to his share, especially since they had become so valuable. And the old man passed the rest of his days in comparative ease, without ever knowing that the stock came from Jim Keene's personal fortune.

There is another side of Jim Keene that has made him a big figure in the minds of the American public. This is his career as a turfman. Keene loved racing for the sake of the race. He maintained one of the greatest breeding stables in the country at Castleton, Kentucky. Moreover, he bred winners. There are few who remember the halcyon days of racing who do not recall the success of Keene's greatest horse, Sysonby. Also the feats of such horses as Domino, Colin, Superman, Maskette, Sweep, Peter Pan, and others from the Keene racing stables.

And here the master mind played. Keene could be seen at the races when his horses were running, always with derby hat and field glasses and absorbing interest in his hobby. In 1881 his horse *They say in Wall Street that he was the biggest.* Foxhall won the Grand Prix at Paris, and he was almost as well known on the English turf as on the American racetracks. In 1907 his winnings on his horses aggregated half a million dollars – a small sum, perhaps, to him, but a triumph to his success in breeding horses.

He believed the sport should be kept clean, and to his efforts was due much of the eradication of the evils that had sprung up around the "sport of kings."

One might imagine that Keene's vocabulary was the list of securities traded in on the market. Quite the contrary. He was widely read in science, art, and literature. He had the broad view of world affairs and the narrower view of the tape accurately synchronized.

Jim Keene died shortly before the big war market took place. They say in Wall Street that he was the biggest figure that has ever existed in his particular field. His was the master hand that pulled the wires, that made railroad heads, bank presidents, captains of industry move like automatons. When Keene acted, the market was likely to boil over. He had a tremendous following. If it happened to leak out that Keene was buying, the Street followed him blindly because Keene was usually successful. He was daring, but, like a good general, he knew when to retreat. He was aggressive, but never to the point of foolhardiness. He was reticent – but in his reticence was his success. It has been said that there will never be another Jim Keene. But already a contemporary is beginning to fill his shoes – of which, more at another time.

JAY GOULD

Jay Gould, probably the greatest operator in railroad securities in the financial history of America, was a constructionist. He took failures and made them successes.

Clever, forceful, and daring, he forms an heroic-size figure in the development of the transportation systems of the country. Gould was a creator, not a speculator. His fortune, won by his courage, was created wealth.

JAY GOULD

The everlasting monument of one of the most forceful, courageous, and daring stock market operators is the so-called
"Gould System" of railroads. Jay Gould, at the time of his death,
passed on as a heritage, a well organized system of railroads, won
in a series of "battles of titans" on the floor of the New York Stock
Exchange. Perhaps some of the methods used by Gould and his
contemporaries can never be repeated in Stock Exchange history,
because of ever-changing conditions, both in Stock Exchange dealings and in publicity, but no matter what those methods may have
been, the fact that Gould left a well organized system of railroads
and a fortune of $75,000,000 to his heirs, all of which was created
by amazing fertility of mind and force of character, must command
the respect of the world.

Gould started with nothing save the good blood back of him.
His father was a farmer, but a descendant of Abraham Gould, a
lieutenant-colonel in the Continental army, so that we find the
name of Gould in the foundations of American history. Jay Gould
was born at Stratton's Falls, Delaware County, N.Y. in 1836.
There is no question, from the remarks of Gould himself in later
life, but that his early years were those of the farm drudgery that
usually befell the lot of a farmer's boy. But we find that master
mind, which was later to become one of the big forces of the
financial world, reaching out beyond his small horizon, and at

fifteen, he was working in a tinsmith's shop; at sixteen he was a partner in the business.

It is evident that, during this time, an inherent love of mathematics began to creep to the surface, finding its outlet in a taste for civil engineering and surveying. He devoured all the books available on the subject and, having secured a good groundwork, started out vigorously on the practical end of the profession. Gould's first place in this business was as an assistant to a surveyor in Ulster County for "$20 a month and found." There is no doubt that Gould had application, and, while a surveyor, wrote histories of Ulster, Sullivan, and Greene Counties. The sale of his books and maps brought him in about $5,000. With this stake, he joined Zadock Pratt in establishing a tannery in Pennsylvania. In 1859, Gould bought out Pratt's interest and turned over the tannery at a substantial profit.

In 1862, he married the daughter of Daniel G. Miller and it is at this point, through his father-in-law, that Gould's interest in railroads and railroad affairs becomes a direct one. Daniel G. Miller was largely interested in the Rensselaer & Saratoga Railroad, which connected Troy and Saratoga. *That battle of the giants – the war between Gould and Vanderbilt.* The road was then practically bankrupt, when Gould stepped in and put it on a basis where he netted three quarters of a million dollars, his first profits from railroad operations.

In his rehabilitation of the Rensselaer & Saratoga and later the Rutland & Washington, running from Troy to Rutland, Vermont, he displayed unusual acumen, not only in developing the earning power of the roads he took hold of, but in making advantageous consolidations and alliances, the seed of the idea that was later to blossom into the "Gould System" of railroads, for Gould unquestionably was a creator. He took hold of the things that other men had failed with and made them useful to the community.

In 1867, we find Gould established as a railroad operator and his success in his early ventures leading him into broader fields. He became attracted to Erie and then began that battle of the giants, which will never be forgotten in financial history – the war between Gould and Vanderbilt.

Gould had already laid the foundations of his fortune. It was here that Gould allied himself with Daniel Drew, a moneylender, and "Jim" Fisk. Vanderbilt then owned the New York Central and saw that if Erie got into the hands of any single interest that could rebuild it, it would prove a dangerous competitor to him. There is no doubt that Vanderbilt and Gould saw the possibilities of Erie very clearly, but Vanderbilt saw them first. Erie was then dominated by Daniel Drew and in 1866, Vanderbilt had bought enough stock to secure control. Drew, Gould, and James Fisk, Jr., who had risen from a peddler in Vermont to a Wall Street broker, determined to wrest control of Erie away from Vanderbilt and in the battle between these giants, Erie went through a period of spectacular price movements, that made it one of the greatest trading issues ever listed on the New York Stock Exchange.

The titanic struggle is one of the most fascinating pages in American financial history.

The battle was fought for three years and there were drawn into it, not only some of the largest financial interests in the country, but banks, judges, and legislatures. The titanic struggle of Gould and his associates with Vanderbilt is one of the most fascinating pages in American financial history. It was fought chiefly on the floor of the New York Stock Exchange and made Gould the greatest market operator of his time.

If Gould were a giant mentally, he was physically the opposite. He was about five feet, six inches high, with a slender figure and seemed to be marked by an excessive timidity. His complexion was swarthy and trimmed black whiskers concealed a substantial portion of his face. His eyes, however, were dark and peculiarly piercing, evidencing the forceful character that lay back of them, while the high forehead suggested the giant mind. His voice was low and insinuating. He dressed usually in black and a heavy gold watch chain adorned his vest. Eye glasses swung from a silk cord around his neck and one noted the little touch of personal vanity in the diamond or ruby set cuff studs.

Gould, in his struggle for Erie, had made money, and was still ambitious. He and his associates in 1869 attempted a corner in gold and although the corner was broken, Gould is estimated to have made $11,000,000 on the attempt. The breaking of the gold corner precipitated a panic in Wall Street affairs, known as "Black Friday," on September 24, 1869, when the prices of securities crashed and at which time, it is stated that Gould stepped in to pick up the bargains. It will be remembered that Gould was then an adept at scenting bargains in railroads and that at heart, as shown from his earlier experiences in the railroads of New York State, he was a constructionist. He had, it is estimated, at the time of the "Black Friday" panic, between $25,000,000 and $30,000,000. With this he went into Union Pacific, to be later disposed of to Harriman in 1890 at a substantial profit. He also acquired Missouri Pacific and with his interest in Wabash, Kansas Pacific, St Louis, Iron Mountain & Southern, St Louis & Southwestern, and Texas Pacific is to be found the beginning of the famous "Gould System."

It looked for a time as though the Gould interests were going to gobble up the entire railroad system of the United States and his acquisition of the western railroads was not to go unchallenged. In 1887, the Pacific Railway Commission held a thorough investigation in New York, Boston, and San Francisco. The *New York Times* of April 27, 1887, commenting on Mr Gould's position in the railroad world, said that it seemed most improbable that Jay Gould had been a railroad magnate of the first class for little more than half a decade. It pointed out that in 1879 he owned only the nucleus of the then big system he controlled and that, through purchase and construction, Gould then owned 6,000 miles of rail. One gets a substantial picture of Gould from the article:

> He has traveled many times over every mile of his railroads. There is an immensity of interest in such a trip when made for the first time, or even the second or third, but it has been made so often by Mr Gould that he has thoroughly absorbed all the pleasure to be obtained from it, except that which smacks of dollars and power. His trips occupy about three weeks from the time his special car, the

"Convoy," leaves St Louis until it returns to that hot and dusty city of pageants and conventions.

When word is flashed to St Louis that Mr Gould is on his way, every official on the system packs his head full of information, and there is unwonted activity from Omaha to Galveston and from Fort Worth to San Antonio. All of the system's executive force was selected either by Mr Gould or by trusted officials in whom he had implicit faith, and the heads of divisions who work for Jay Gould could not work harder for anybody else, although in some instances their bank accounts do not show it.

He is a strong advocate of method. The day's work is laid out in the morning and almost before the train starts in the morning he has settled how many stops can be made during the day and where the night can be spent. He dines and sleeps on board his car from the start to the finish of a three weeks' trip. At night the "Convoy" is run to the quietest part of the yard, as the owner objects to more noise than he can avoid at night, though he can apparently stand as much as anyone else in daylight. His car is always a curiosity along the line, and people come from far and near to look at it as it stands in the evening in a secluded spot, secure in its loneliness. In some parts of the country through which his roads run, he is quite as much of a curiosity in the eyes of the country folk as a circus, and were he to stand on the platform after the manner of James G. Blaine, would attract quite as big a crowd as that gentle man. He is never apparently anxious to achieve notoriety in that way, and is quite as modest in his demeanor while on one of his tours as he is in his office or his Fifth Avenue mansion. In the latter, as a few newspaper reporters know, he is more unassuming and far more polite than a majority of his thousand dollar employees.

As a further insight into Mr Gould's personality, the *Philadelphia Press* once told a story of his first yachting experience, in which Gould was forced to put on a pair of overalls in order to protect broadcloth trousers from paint which had become baked and chalky. The overalls had been obtained by a friend of his by the name of Cruger from a storekeeper in Peekskill. When the party returned to Peekskill, Gould, without a word to Cruger, resold the overalls to the storekeeper. Cruger determined to play a practical joke on Gould and knowing that he had to keep a business engagement, involving quite a sum of money, staged a grounding of the boat within 50 feet of the Ossining railroad station, where Mr Could was to catch his train.

An eye-witness tells the rest of the story, showing the tremendous amount of determination in the composure of the saturnine little man:

Already the train was in sight, two miles away, and whatever was to be done had to be done quickly. As I have said, there was plenty of grit in the embryo railroad king, and quick as a wink he was out of his sable clothes and standing before us, clad only in his aggressively scarlet undergarments. Holding his precious broadcloth suit above his head, he stepped into the water, which, shallow as it was, reached to the armpits of the little gentleman. Then he started for the shore, his short, thin legs working back and forth in a most comical fashion as he strove to quicken his pace. The station platform was crowded with people, and very soon the strange figure approaching them was descried. A peal of laughter from 500 throats rolled over the water to us, the ladies hiding their blushes behind parasols and fans. The men shouted with laughter. Finally the wader reached the base on the stone wall, and for a moment covered with confusion – and but little else – stood upon the rock, one scarlet leg uplifted, looking for all the world like a flamingo on the shore of a Florida bayou, while the air was split with shrieks of laughter, in which we now unreservedly joined. Then came the climax of the joke, which nearly paralyzed the unfortunate victim.

"Haul on your sheets, boys, and up with the board!" was Cruger's order. As the yacht gathered headway and swept by within ten feet of the astonished Mr Gould, we laughingly bade him good-bye, advising a warm mustard bath when he got home.

Then his quick mind took in the full force of the practical joke we had worked upon him and his dark face was a study for a painter. But the train had already reached the station, taken on its passengers and the wheels were beginning to turn again for its run to the city. As Gould scrambled up the wall, his glossy black suit still pressed affectionately to his bosom, the "All aboard!" had sounded and the cars were moving. Every window was filled with laughing faces as he raced over the sand and stones and was dragged by two brakemen on the rear platform, panting and dripping. The last glimpse we caught of him was as the train entered the prison tunnel. Then, supported on either side by the railroad men, he was making frantic plunges in his efforts to thrust his streaming legs into his trousers as the platform reeled and rocked beneath him.

Mr Gould created wealth rather than gained money by speculation. It was his purpose to turn failure to success, to make dollars grow rather than to attempt to get the dollar of the other fellow. He had faith in the future as he had faith in himself and following his success in the railroads, turned his attention to the telegraph company. Under Gould, the American Telegraph Co. laid an Atlantic cable and broke down the monopoly, forcing the amalgamation with the Western Union Telegraph Co. with Gould as the chief stockholder.

He also acquired control of the Elevated Railway in New York City, rebuilding as formerly, run down properties into well paying organizations.

Gould died in 1892, leaving some $75,000,000 to six children. Single handed, Jay Gould carved his way to fame as a construc-*A market operator of exceptional ability.* tionist and as a market operator of exceptional ability. Like the broken steel that goes into the melting pot to regain its lost temper, so Jay Gould took the broken railroads and remade them into transportation systems that form big links in the carrier systems of the United States today.

There will probably never arise anyone who will dispute his title as "the greatest operator in railroad securities in the financial history of the United States."

BERNARD M. BARUCH

Equipped with a "sound mind in a sound body,"
Bernard Mannes Baruch is the stock market operator
in Wall Street of the writers of romance.
His magnificent manhood, his handsome face, his
inscrutable smile denote a personality that forms a
complement to that master mind that has raised him to
the pinnacle of success, not only in Wall Street, but in
Washington.

BERNARD M. BARUCH

Imagine him! Six-feet-two, albeit slim for his height, yet with the chest of a blacksmith. Well knit, muscular, a veritable giant in physique – the complement of the giant mind that makes him one of the leading figures in Wall Street – Bernard M. Baruch.

Look into his clean-shaven, good-looking face, with the ever-present smile. Observe that intensity of concentration in his forehead and you will see the character that has made Baruch one of the financial powers of the present generation of market operators.

For Bernard M. Baruch is, at this writing, only 52 years of age – physically and mentally in his prime. True, he is no longer active in the market, but his sphere has broad-

Baruch is the living embodiment of the Wall Street operator.

ened. He has become a figure of national importance and may gain even greater fame in new fields than that attained as a market operator.

Baruch is the living embodiment of the Wall Street operator created by the novelists and playwrights. Or conversely if you wish, the fictional characters were made in the image of Baruch. He is affable, urbane, suave. He will talk freely about himself, but not about his operations in the market.

The workings of Baruch's mind have never been visible. That it is a master mind is apparent from his success, not only in the market, but in the manner in which he conducted the work, assigned to him by Woodrow Wilson, in World War I. One suspects that mentally he is a superman. Intuition, "hunch," and premonition seem to be as potent forces in arriving at his conclusions as logic. It would seem, sometimes, as though he had three or four extra senses to aid Reason.

And yet he is humble. He has never fallen into the quicksand of egotism and, although his success pleases him, it is always a source of wonder to him. His enemies are few, chiefly because he lacks the egotism to create them.

Baruch opened his eyes on August 19, 1870, in Camden, S.C. He was the second son born to Dr and Mrs Simon Baruch. Two more came after Bernard, so that he was one of four. His father settled in South Carolina in 1856 and tried to become a small businessman, but with ill success. Turning to medicine, he literally educated himself and began practicing in Camden. But when the Civil War broke out, he enlisted in Lee's army, winning the admiration and respect of the great general of the Confederacy. The souvenirs and mementos of Dr Baruch's friendship with Lee are among the most treasured possessions of the Baruchs.

His mother was Miss Isabel Wolfe, a charming sample of southern womanhood and the daughter of a planter. The sympathies of the Baruchs are distinctly with the South, a factor that may have had some slight influence in Bernard M. Baruch's selection by President Wilson to one of the more important posts in the "war cabinet."

In early years the foundations of his splendid character were laid

by his father and mother, who enjoined him to the strict performance of his duty as a citizen and that the single outstanding principle
of an American should be scrupulous honesty. When, later in life,
Bernard became a broker, he placed on his desk, in sight of all, a
photograph of his father with this wise admonition: "Let unswerv-
ing integrity always be your guide." The photograph is always the
principal ornament of Mr Baruch's desk wherever he may be.

Young Baruch was first educated in a private school. When the
family moved to New York, in 1881, Bernard was put into a
public school and later entered the college of the city of New
York, from which he was graduated, and it was during his college
career that he evidently became attracted to business and finance,
supplementing his studies by prodigious reading at home on the
subjects that had begun to fascinate him. No doubt his father
wondered what there could be in the dry "manuals" and voluminous statistics that could attract the youth.

After his graduation, his first "job" was that with a firm of deal-
ers in druggists' supplies at three dollars a week. Three or four
months convinced him that there were little or no possibilities for
advancement. The story is related that a phrenologist told his
mother that the "bumps" showed the boy had an unusual ability
for organization and was a born financier, and it was her ambitious
nature that brought young Bernard in touch with the financial
editor of one of the leading newspapers of New York, which connection led to his being given employment in a brokerage office.

He found his field. The heads of the firm recognized instantly
that young Baruch had a decided leaning toward brokerage and

speculation. His talent for securing the regard and confidence of men then powerful in the financial world was amazing. The firm had big customers like James R. Keene, Edwin Hawley, and the Guggenheims and young Baruch worked hard and won the confidence of these men simultaneously. His salary began to climb.

It was not long before the firm, keenly aware of the young man's unusual ability, his well kept tongue, and his unimpeachable *The magnitude of his* integrity that had been ingrained in his *trades could sway the* nature by his wise father, gave him a *whole market.* place in their organization and he practically became a member of the firm. It was while in this position that he conducted big market operations for Keene and other big and successful operators.

But it is said of Mr Baruch that never in his associations of this character did he take advantage of the information that he had, although the personal use of it might have gained him a comfortable fortune. Not even his family had the slightest inkling of the confidences between himself and his clients.

It was natural that he should rapidly become big enough to "sail his own boat" and in 1899 he bought a seat and entered a remarkable career as a market operator.

It was then that his remarkable mental gifts of almost uncanny intuition and foresight, his knowledge of the market, brought him fame and success. For Baruch was a big operator. The very magnitude of his trades could sway the whole market and he had as a guiding factor a broad perspective of economics and finance, of the nation's business, of world affairs. He was able to translate events and conditions into terms of future security prices.

He made millions, he lost millions, and he made millions again. And through all his operations he was elusive, secretive, shadowy – the workings of that master mind were never revealed and probably never will be. It may be that the secret of his success cannot be reduced to terms of simple reasoning. What part intuition played, probably even Mr Baruch himself may not know.

Subsequent to 1901, Mr Baruch was interested in momentous transactions in securities with Keene, Ryan, Harriman, the Guggenheims, Hawley, and others. Baruch was the right hand man at various times of these financial and market leaders. It was the time of the huge consolidations, a broadening out of American business and financial affairs – the time of the setting of new standards of capitalization of corporations. His dependability led the Guggenheims to send him west to buy copper mines. Thomas F. Ryan commissioned him to acquire tobacco companies and Hawley to investigate and buy railroad organizations.

In the performance of these tasks, he was entrusted with hundreds of millions of dollars and not only did these men trust Baruch, but they admired and liked him. He had ability plus personality.

Bernard M. Baruch was a big figure in financial affairs when World War I broke out. He was likewise a devoted admirer of Woodrow Wilson and his policies and it was unquestionably his dependability, his power of organization, that led Wilson, in 1916, to appoint him a member of the Advisory Committee of the Council of National Defense. He had the confidence of the

President and the manner in which he brought order out of chaos led to the chairmanship of the Committee on Raw Material, Minerals and Metals and his appointment as Commissioner-in-Charge of Purchasing for the War Industries Board. In 1918, he became chairman of the War Industries Board, resigning from that position on January 1, 1919, and was appointed one of the American Commissioners to Negotiate Peace. Later he was appointed American Delegate on Economic and Reparations Agreements and economic adviser at the Paris Peace Conference. The tale of Baruch's activities on behalf of America during the war, of supplying the armies with the things that carried the conflict to its successful conclusion, would fill a big book in itself.

In his work in Washington he showed that remarkable trait that characterizes leadership. He surrounded himself with the best men he could find – and trusted them implicitly. It is one of his rules. He trusts men until he finds they cannot be trusted.

And he gave the men that aided him the highest credit. He never tired of praising Legg, Replogle, Summers, and others. About his own work he was modest. But he inspired in his associates that which makes for success in the building of any organization, whether it be political, business, or otherwise – loyalty.

During the war, William Allen White, the famous editor of the *Emporia Gazette*, drew the following portrait in a paragraph of Bernard M. Baruch. He said:

> The leader of the group is Bernard Baruch, six feet two, trim, keen, open-faced, gray-eyed, candid as to countenance, quick-moving, decisive, friendly, resourceful and as little satisfied as a handsome

man dare be. He is the newer type of American Jew. American life has pressed almost the last vestige of his blood from his mien. It is a strong blood, but this is a strong civilization we are making here, and in Baruch we see the two forces grappling with one another. And the Western civilization is fairly well prevailing. But he has all the high vision that his blood entitles him to, all the capacity for honorable compromise, the ability to put himself in the other man's place. He is facile, gentle and has tremendous personal charm. He leads by charm rather than by force, as David must have led of old.

Mark Sullivan, the noted Washington newspaper correspondent and national observer of men and measures, sums up his opinion of the personality of the subject of this sketch as follows:

To my personal equation, Baruch is most engaging, not when he is functioning in the manner of his greatest ability, not when he is in the role of executive, hustling about and getting things done. When he interests me most is in the role of reflective philosopher. I know few better ways of spending an afternoon than to be in the country with Baruch, where things don't clamor at his attention and when his mind will run along without any guide and his reflections will flow out of his mouth as spontaneously and as irregularly as water out of a spring. On such an afternoon I have heard him talk about old age, religion, clubs, poverty, dancing, money, snobbishness, prize-fighting, greed, boarding houses, gambling, children, politics, ambitions – to say nothing of his comments based on the shrewdest and most penetrating and generally most sympathetic understanding of public men. On such an afternoon of leisure and in such a role, Baruch is a combination of Walt Mason, Dr Samuel Johnson and the less ascetic aspects of Epictetus.

Baruch's future is a matter of great speculation. He has said that he is through with Wall Street. He has been heard to say many times that he resolved to quit business because he learned so much *It is felt that Mr Baruch* as head of the War Industries Board, *is destined for even* that it would be improper for him ever *greater things.* to go into the market again. He said, however, once before, that he was out of the market "for keeps." But he came back. Perhaps he may again feel the call. Who knows? But, it is felt that Mr Baruch is destined for even greater things. He has demonstrated a capability for public service that cannot go unrecognized. Perhaps high honors are still in store for him. Certainly he has the capabilities and it is inconceivable that his remarkable mental equipment should rust.

Much has been said regarding the Baruch smile. But there is more of a smile in the gray eyes which look, as one of his biographers puts it, "as though he knew a good joke that he was keeping to himself."

He is a fluent talker. He likes to move about and often he talks about himself. But it is not conceit. It is but the natural pride of the successful man. He is a tireless worker and his enthusiasms are great. He applies himself with whole hand and heart to the task to which he assigns himself. In his work for the government, he applied himself with the characteristic vigor that made him a leader among stock market operators, and in the broader fields of public service, that characteristic dominates him – one that may make him a national leader as he was a giant in Wall Street.

THOMAS W. LAWSON

"Tom" Lawson, author, financier, farmer, yachtsman,
turfman, horticulturist, is probably one of the most
interesting figures in current financial affairs.
Words are Lawson's playthings. He might bear on his
esutcheon, the copy-book maxim, "The pen is mightier
than the sword." But the militant words that have
emanated from the fertile mind of the Boston genius
bear a closer resemblance to the more powerful
instruments of modern warfare.
Lawson's methods are unique. He has always stood
where the sun can shine fully on him. And the sun
shines on a remarkable and lovable personality.

THOMAS W. LAWSON

One wonders what the opinion of the Man in the Street is of Thomas W. Lawson. That is to say, the impression of the man who knows not the real Lawson, but one whose knowledge of him has been gained from his voluminous writings, from those who have discussed him in the public print, from the utterances of both his enemies and his friends. Do they think of him as the Don Quixote de la Mancha of the financial world?

But Don Quixote was sincere, if militant. And if the public, viewing Lawson's stormy career, characterize him as the Knight of the Financial Windmills, let no one question Lawson's sincerity of purpose in a belief that he was jousting with hydra-headed monsters.

One cannot conceive that it is all a pose. One reads what he has *Lawson is the antithesis* written and the note of sincerity sounds *of the average stock* through it. Even the flagrant ballyhoo, *market operator.* crimson-inked "tissues" breathe the sincerity of the man who penned them. For Lawson is the antithesis of the average stock market operator. They cloak their operations. Lawson, figuratively, stands on the street corner with a brass band, telling about his.

They flit through the night. Lawson comes out in the open, selects the biggest lot in town, puts up the tent, and invites the public to a free show. The average stock market operator conceals what he is doing from the public. Lawson tells the world what he is doing and invites the public to help him. And, whereas the average stock market operator shrinks from publicity and repels a would-be following, Lawson focusses upon himself thousands of spotlights, that all may see what he is doing.

Lawson the Author, Lawson the Breeder, Lawson the Horticulturist, Lawson the Yachtsman, Lawson the Dog Fancier, Lawson the Turfman. Lawson the Farmer, Lawson the Enemy of "the System," Beau Brummel Lawson – all these are but spotlights on Lawson, the Financier.

He is a familiar figure in Boston. One cannot mention Young's Hotel without conjuring up the figure of Thomas W. Lawson with the inevitable carnation in his buttonhole. Bostonians know him – and love him.

Thomas W. Lawson, like many other great living Americans, was born poor. He first saw the light of day on February 26, 1857 in Charlestown. His boyhood was spent in East Cambridge, and in his school days developed the militant spirit that has characterized his career. He loved a fight and he would fight fair if the other fellow did. He has always done so. As long as the other side was fighting fair, Lawson would not break the rules. But let the rules be swept aside and Lawson would play the same game the other fellow did.

At the age of 12, his ambition came bubbling to the surface and seeing a sign, "Boy Wanted," in a banking house in State Street, hired himself out for $3 a week. He went home and told his mother and she promptly sent him back to school. But with the aid of the men in the banking house, his mother was won over and he started on that memorable career of finance, the center of which has rarely been further than a rifle shot from the place where he obtained his first position.

It must have been in his blood, for almost immediately young Lawson was attracted to speculation in securities. We find him, at an early age, figuring out a rebound in a railroad stock that had been severely depressed, buying at $3 a share and selling at $16. On the heels of it – and Lawson still in his teens – we see him a leader in a pool in Boston Water Power stock and going broke, after which he took $159 – all he had in the world – and gave a dinner to his associates in the pool at Young's Hotel, presenting the last five dollar bill to the head waiter. For years Lawson made his headquarters at Young's. He got the habit in his early days of lunching at the hotel and he has been taking lunch at Young's ever since. In fact, his three rooms in the hotel were, for many years, his business headquarters.

For Lawson is a veritable master of words, words with a punch in them stronger than Jack Dempsey's wicked left!

Lawson's spirit could not, however, be crushed by simply "going broke" and, in a short time, he had five figures to his credit in the bank. From modest operations, Lawson went into larger ones, until one finds him in early manhood, with the capabilities of a Keene, a Cammack, or a White – but with methods of his own.

At an early stage of his career, he recognized the value of advertising, whether it be advertising his wares or advertising himself. In fact, Lawson may be said to have been one of the pioneers of advertising and publicity as we know it today.

For Lawson is a veritable master of words, a general of well organized armies of words – words soft and bland, barbed words, blunt words and pointed words, words that are sweeter than honey, words that are tipped with vitriol, words softer than swansdown and words with a punch in them stronger than Jack Dempsey's wicked left! And when he lacked a word, he coined a new one – a Lawsonesque word, but always the right word!

Lawson's early financial career was nothing if not spectacular. He was in and out of all sorts of sensational things, including dragging Westinghouse out of a big hole. He was associated with H. H. Rogers in stock market operations aggregating $100,000,000. It was while with Rogers that Lawson made his first big fortune, which, it is estimated, aggregated between $8,000,000 and $9,000,000. Shortly followed the writing of *Frenzied Finance*. His motives in writing it were chiefly to reform American business and financial methods and to make money – that is to increase the number of investors and speculators who would join him in market campaigns.

The last phrase explains something of Lawson's methods and his attitude toward the public. For Lawson believes in the strength of unified action. He knows that simultaneous buying of one thousand or ten thousand individuals can raise the market price of a security in a spectacular manner, and, when in a market campaign, he endeavors to polarize public buying, knowing that with his own forces, the united and concerted purchasing will have a tremendous influence upon prices.

Frank Fayant, one of the most brilliant of the country's financial writers, wrote of Lawson, back in 1907:

No unprejudiced reader of Lawson's life-story can deny that the man has an extraordinarily brilliant mind. The writer, in doing his journalistic day's work, has had to brush elbows with many brilliant men – the men whose stature places them conspicuously above their fellows – statesmen, scholars, scientists, physicians, explorers, judges, railroad builders, empire-makers – and Lawson ranks as one of the brilliant men of his times . . .

With his brilliancy go hand in hand his energy and enthusiasm. His energy is amazing. Not one man in a thousand can keep pace with him. He has a multiple-cylinder, high-speed mind. His enthusiasm is equally amazing. To form a clear conception of the man, his enthusiasm must always be taken account of. He is enthusiastic over everything that occupies his mind – whether it be a design for a door-knocker at Dreamworld, or a remedy for a worldwide panic; and he is enthusiastic over himself – his career, his work, his mental power, his plan of revolutionizing the social order . . .

And one other thing – through the man's whole make-up runs a great big vein of sentiment. He has a heart as big as his head. He can cry. For a man of his commanding mental and physical strength, his almost woman-like vein of sentiment is amazing. His love for his home and his children is so great that even his enemies speak of it.

. . . But when Lawson lays bare his heart, as he did in his recent letter to his publishers, referring to the death of his wife ("I saw the dearest of all my possessions go to the grave before her time . . . a life every second of which was dearer to me than anything in this or the next world"), he does it without stopping to think what the world will say.

Of Lawson's relations with copper, nothing stands out so vividly in his career as his championship of the porphyries.* For Lawson believed in the future of the porphyry coppers, believed they were destined to represent the backbone of American copper production. He foresaw the big values that would eventually develop in these new copper mines and his campaign on Chino, in which he advised the purchase of the stock at $5 per share, will long be remembered.

Through advertisements in the public press – and Lawson was no niggard when it came to spending money for advertising – he advised the American public to buy the porphyry coppers, which advice was based on sound economic reasoning. The porphyry

The porphyry coppers have fulfilled every prediction that Mr Lawson made for them.

coppers have fulfilled every prediction that Mr Lawson made for them and he recommended their purchase when they were in a more or less nebulous state financially, since which time they have developed into investments of the highest character.

It is to Thomas W. Lawson's everlasting credit that he was aligned on the constructive side of the American copper industry, as it is today and it was greatly due to his efforts that the American public bought such stocks as Chino, Ray Consolidated,

Editor's note:
* A red stone embedded with crystals.

Inspiration, and Utah and participated in the profits that accrued in the market, as these issues passed from mere prospects into profitable mining industries.

There is an intensely human side to Thomas W. Lawson. His magnificent estate, "Dreamwold" at Egypt, Mass., has been the subject of so much comment that its description need find no place in this chronicle. It is here that Mr Lawson has enjoyed his leisure – such as it has been. For he has been an extremely busy man and an extremely active one.

His breeding of fine cattle, of fine dogs, his growing of fine flowers, which culminated in the purchase of the carnation which bears his name, have all been reported more or less faithfully in the public press of the last 20 years. It is remembered that he built the yacht, *Independence*, at a cost of $200,000 and when it was shut out from the America's Cup race, he smilingly threw it into the scrap heap. It is also remembered that at one time he owned a racing stable, and Lawson pitching hay on his estate at "Dreamwold" has been a familiar figure to New England.

As a poor youngster in State Street, Lawson dreamed of the wonderful estate just outside of Boston, with its stables full of prize horses and cattle and he made that dream come true.

One gets an adequate picture of Mr Lawson at the height of his career through the eyes of James Creelman. Lawson had been telling Creelman of the value of publicity, explaining that it was the most powerful weapon in the world and with it he had been able to strike with some of the power which eight million Americans possess when they are wide awake and in earnest. At that time, Mr Lawson had just spent $92,000 for an advertisement over his signature in New York, Boston, Chicago, and Los Angeles and had cabled the advertisement to London. Mr. Creelman said:

> Mr Lawson stood squarely upon his heels, the incarnation of strength and courage. The square head, high and wide at the top, the long line of the jaw and broad, fighting chin, big blue-gray eyes, the big, flat teeth, the strong nose, large firm mouth, sinewy neck, hairy hands, broad, deep chest, powerfully curved thighs, and the steady voice – these were eloquent of strength, determination, and concentration.

Mr Creelman might have completed the picture by noting that Mr Lawson wore a No. 6 shoe, a No. 5 glove – and an eight-and-three-quarters hat!

Lawson is militant. As a boy he loved a fight. As this chronicle is written, he is 65 and all through his career that love of the fight – as well as his love of fame – has been undimmed. We find him at times in the forefront of battle, alternated with periods of absolute retirement. As this is written, the spirit of Thomas W. Lawson is absent from the Street. But tomorrow may find him in the lists again, courageous, earnest, valiantly shouting: "Lay on, MacDuff."

Those who have known Thomas W. Lawson love him and admire him, first for those essentially human qualities which have endeared him to thousands of friends throughout New England and, second, for his fearlessness, his willingness to call things by their right names, and the magic of his word jugglery.

JOHN W. GATES

*True type of American hustler, "Bet-a-Million" Gates,
with his dynamic energy forms one of the most
interesting figures in American financial history.
Gates's market success was built upon a belief in
America and belief in himself. He was ever a "bull,"
always a force on the constructive side. Gates
demonstrated that barbed wire would hold wild steers,
but nothing was ever found to hold Gates, whenever
he started a market campaign.*

JOHN W. GATES

....

To write of John W. Gates, without referring to his frequent offers to "bet-a-million," would be like attempting to tell the story of Hamlet, with the Prince of Denmark left out. It stands as a symbol of the man, not a symbol of recklessness – as many of the younger generation believe – but the embodiment of forcefulness and conviction, backed up by the largest money unit of his time.

For John W. Gates was one of the greatest "bulls" in America. He believed in the country, he believed in the country's business, and he believed in himself. And the man who believes in himself and backs up that belief by seven figures is entitled to respect.

Next time you see a barbed wire fence, picture to yourself the part it has played in the development of America and say to your-*For John W. Gates was* self that, if it hadn't been for John W. *one of the greatest* Gate's dynamic, forceful personality *"bulls" in America.* and belief in barbed wire fences, it might have taken an additional 20 years to overcome the prejudice against them.

And when you look at the position the United States Steel Corporation occupies in the world today, remember that John W. Gates was a factor in putting together this giant of all American industrial enterprises.

Contemporary of Keene, the Moores, Reid, Yoakum, and

Harriman, Gates was one of the group of brilliant market operators, financiers, and empire builders that came out of the west. Gates had the country-wide viewpoint. He saw the vision of industrial expansion and supremacy. He was a constructive force in the market of the highest type. His was the hand that built market values by developing earning power.

John Warne Gates was born near Turner Junction, now West Chicago, Ill., in 1855. His father was a farmer and, from all accounts, Gates's early life was little different from that of the

Gates was one of the group of brilliant market operators, financiers, and empire builders.

average farmer's boy. He attended Wheaton College and was graduated from Northwestern College, but if he was a farmer's son, he wasn't lacking in business acumen. Thus, at the age of 16, he entered into a contract to husk a neighboring farmer's corn, earning sufficient to purchase a third interest in a threshing machine. In another year, he was the sole owner of the threshing machine and, at 18, he had $1,000 in the bank – and the threshing machine – sufficient worldly goods, in his opinion, to marry on.

More money was made by an investment in a hardware store, when he came in contact with Colonel Elwood, who had acquired the right to manufacture barbed wire from the inventor, a Missouri blacksmith. Elwood knew the possibilities of barbed wire, but evidently lacked salesmanship ability. And he saw in young Gates enthusiasm and forcefulness, the things needed to introduce barbed wire to the country.

Gates agreed to go to Texas for $25 a week and sell barbed

wire. When he got to Texas, the cattlemen laughed at him. With cyclonic energy, Gates built a corral of barbed wire in San Antonio and invited the cattlemen to turn loose the wildest steers they had. The cattle rushed the fence and came off much worse for the encounter. It was a masterful stroke on the part of Gates and sold practically every cattleman in Texas to barbed wire. Gates sold barbed wire from one end of the state to the other. His sales were enormous, and he then asked Elwood for a partnership. Elwood refused.

With characteristic forcefulness, Gates built a plant of his own and made Elwood come to him for a consolidation. Gates steadily became a factor in the wire industry until, at the formation of the United States Steel Corporation, he was the dominant figure in the business. Without the Gates plants, the Steel Corporation would have been incomplete.

Gates was the true type of American hustler. When he went after a thing, he usually got it. The magnitude of the wire business could not help but bring him to Wall Street. He was practically always committed to the bull side of the market and, because of his constructive attitude, built up a tremendous public following.

The aggressiveness of Gates is demonstrated in a story told by Isaac F. Marcosson some years ago, regarding Gates's coup in Louisville & Nashville:

> He had learned from a Kentuckian that there was enough Louisville & Nashville in the open market to acquire control. With characteristic impetuosity, Gates, in a single day, acquired enough stock to wrest control from the Belmont interests.

When J. P. Morgan heard of this coup, he sent for Mr Gates and said: "Gates, you are not the kind of a man to control L. & N."

"All right!" replied Gates, "Get someone better – with the price!"

Mr Morgan did get someone else and Gates is said to have cleared $4,000,000 on the deal. That is the way he works as the type of aggressive speculator.

Gates knew values. He knew how latent values could be converted into tangible wealth with organization and abundant money. Gates would pick up a drooping corporation, see that it had plenty of funds, and then throw his big, forceful personality into the company's affairs and make it a huge success. Naturally, as the success was attained, the value of the stock increased steadily and the friends of John W. Gates are said to have made a great deal of money in following his fortunes.

It has been said of Gates that he never tried to sneak through the crowd. He always pushed his broad shoulders up against them, making a way for himself and for his followers. As instancing this characteristic of Mr Gates, he noticed in 1898 the possibilities of Colorado Fuel & Iron. He picked up big blocks of the stock in the market cheap and had himself made a director. He helped the management borrow millions in Chicago and made them spend every cent of it in huge steel mills. Gates endeavored to get control of Colorado Fuel & Iron, but was unsuccessful – as unsuccessful as E. H. Harriman was a short time later.

About the time Harriman was trying to get Colorado Fuel & Iron, Gates had become interested in Tennessee Coal & Iron.

Gates's broad vision is clearly shown in his remarks as to what he planned to do with Tennessee Coal & Iron. He said:

> We will spend some $15,000,000 to $25,000,000 on improvement. We will have the money – the sinews of war – to make everything as good as it can be. This campaign of improvement will last for years more. It will take nerve and cash, but we have both. Why shouldn't we develop that property? We have a billion tons of coal. We have enough ore to last a couple of centuries. All we have to do is to put our house in order and go ahead.

That was ever Gates's idea. Get on the right track, push through, jam through, crowd through, with every ounce of energy possible – but get there. And it was these tactics that won Gates his tremendous success. In his stock market operations, he used his resources to the limit. When Gates went into a thing, he went into it lock, stock, and barrel. And there was about as much chance of stopping him as halting a steam roller.

One of the characteristics that seems common to nearly all stock market operators is a remarkable memory. Gates had what one of his biographers calls an "intermittent memory." One gets an intimate picture of this failing in the following article, written in 1904:

> Once he put a check for $1,250,000 in his pocket and carried it around for three days. Then the drawers, in order to make their balance clear, reminded him of the check. In 1902, after astonishing Europe, he landed in New York, full of barbaric pearls and gold. On a dog collar of pearls and diamonds he paid a duty of $6,000. He was going away rejoicing when the deputy collector, who had

taken his declaration, asked to see him alone. "Mr Gates, have you a pearl necklace worth about $35,000 about you?" Mr Gates grinned, acknowledged the necklace and that he had never paid duty on it. His candor cost him $21,000. He had forgotten the necklace.

Another intensely American characteristic of John W. Gates was his love of pie. In fact, Gates was a connoisseur of pie. No matter how much the name savors of comic opera, he had in his office a telegraph operator by the name of Pymacker. Pymacker usually brought a slab of pie to lunch with him and Gates, spotting the piece of pie one day, appropriated it. It was Pie with a capital "P." Gates wanted more of such Pie and, learning that it was made by Mrs Pymacker, had her make for him a nice, juicy lemon pie.

It must have been the King of The Pies, for Gates, as a reward for Mrs Pymacker's industry, sent her 100 shares of Northern Pacific. This was just before the corner in Northern Pacific and might have made her everlasting fortune, but it is sad to relate that Mrs Pymacker sold the stock the next day. However, that wasn't Gates's fault.

Once, during Gates's career, he practically cornered corn. His operations at one point, brought practically every high priced

Once, during Gates's career, he practically cornered corn.

reporter into his office. They were all met by the stubborn fact that Mr Gates was in the inside office and could not be disturbed, and it looked as though something even more important was growing, until his son, Charles, came out and told the reporters, "He is eating pumpkin pie in the inside office."

In 1907, Gates, finding no outlet for his tremendous energy as an appendage of the United States Steel Corporation, turned back to Texas, the scene of his first success, and became interested in the oil fields in the southwestern part of the state. Here, again, his resourcefulness and creative energy were turned loose with the result that the Texas Co. sprang into being and, under his masterly administration, became the largest independent oil company in the country, which it remains today.

Port Arthur, Texas, owes its growth to a modern city of 20,000 to John W. Gates. Port Arthur today handles nearly half the export tonnage of Texas. The Mary Gates hospital and the Port Arthur College are benefactions of Mr and Mrs Gates to the city. In fact, it may be said that Port Arthur exists by virtue of the Texas Refining Co. and the Gulf Refining Co., both Gates enterprises.

If Gates was a good money maker, he was also a good money spender. Like many of the steel barons, he was a patron of art and had an unusually fine gallery in his New York apartment, which included the paintings of Corot, Daubigny, Reynolds, Gainsborough, Rembrandt, and Rubens. Money to him was made to spend, not to hoard.

And Gates knew the power of money. He knew how to concentrate the power of his money, as he knew how to concentrate his mental forces. This is clearly shown in his market operations. When Gates was buying, the market was literally bombarded with buying orders. They did not come out piecemeal. That character-istic partly explains why a Gates market was a spectacular one. The sheer force of the man and money combined was sufficient to draw to it the added force of the buying public, to say nothing of other market constructionists.

Gates's operations in the market represent some of the most *Perhaps therein lay the* interesting in financial history, simply *great success of this* because of their huge open driving *remarkable personality.* force. When Gates started to buy he never stopped until he got what he went after. And he rarely failed.

Gates was a man of many friends. He started as but a drum-mer* of barbed wire in Texas. It has been said that Gates's success was due to the fact that he started as he did. As one of his com-mentators puts it:

He matriculated at the great American school, the "Drummer's university." Its graduates know the manner of many men and cities. They see the country and grow up with it. They hold familiar con-verse with all sorts of people. They know all stories, all railroad routes, all hotels, all tricks of all trades, all games and principally poker. Accidents, explosions, earthquakes, floods, fires, chorus girls, terrapin, fried pork – all varieties and episodes build in them the philosophical mind. They are surprised by nothing. They are afraid of nothing. They take their chance and jump at every good opportunity.

Perhaps therein lay the great success of this remarkable

Editor's note:
* A favorite word in nineteenth-century America for what we would today call a "traveling salesman."

personality. He was a staunch friend and a good enemy. His philosophy had evolved from much contact with his fellowmen. He died in Paris in 1911, leaving a heritage of memory to the ambitious youth of America.

ROSWELL P. FLOWER

A plain man – a man of the people – in whom the confidence of thousands rested. At one time he came close to getting the highest honors of the land. Always a constructionist, the "Flower market" at the close of the last century, created by the rampant optimism of one of the most interesting figures the Street has ever seen, advanced securities values five billions of dollars in one year.

ROSWELL P. FLOWER

E ach of the Wall Street operators is a type. As one analyzes their methods of market operations, it is realized that no single characteristic is to be found that may be established as a key to their success. Some work in the light, some in the dark; some with tremendous concentrated energy, some by that persistent effort that, like drops of water, wears away the stone. Some love publicity; some shun it. Some call the resources of their friends to their aid; some work alone.

Nor are personal characteristics any common factor. It is a far cry from the frail Harriman to the burly Gates, from the ignorance

Roswell P. Flower was one of the most picturesque figures Wall Street has ever known. of Daniel Drew to the erudition of Bernard Baruch or from the almost courtly Keene to the ultra-commoner type of Roswell P. Flower. Yet each, partly through his methods, partly through his personal characteristics, built up a following, built for himself success.

Roswell P. Flower was one of the most picturesque figures Wall Street has ever known. He was plain – of the plain people. Moreover, he was a bull. His methods were openly constructive and because he made one of the greatest bull markets the Street had ever seen – made hundreds of thousands of dollars for his friends – his is a memory that the annalist of the Street may not ignore.

The rise of Brooklyn Rapid Transit in the Flower boom of 1898 and 1899, which lifted with it practically every security on the list, stands out as one of the most remarkable constructive market operations in the history of the Street – and one of the most profitable for the trading public.

In studying the history of the men who have been successful in Wall Street, one is struck somewhat by the number of those who were farmer's lads. Do they draw something from the soil in their early days that later is transmuted into courage or exceptional acumen, or an ability to handle the tokens of wealth? Roswell P. Flower was not a farmer s son, but in his early days, worked on a farm. He was born in Theresa, Jefferson County, New York, in 1835. Roswell was the sixth of nine children and when his father died was but eight years old. With his brothers, he worked on two farms owned by his mother and, together with odd jobs in a brickyard and at other places in the village, managed to obtain sufficient funds to put himself through school, graduating from the village high school in 1851.

Before he was seventeen years old he had been a teacher in a district school and, if the gossip of the community is to be believed, the scholars were unruly, which unruliness Flower promptly squelched by stern physical measures rather than gentle persuasion.

We find him learning the value of money, beginning with his appointment as assistant postmaster of Watertown, N.Y. in 1854. Here he received a salary of $600 a year which sounds small, but $600 went a long way in those days. Out of his salary he purchased a half interest in a jewelry store and in two years he bought out his partner.

His first association with Wall Street came in 1869 when Henry Keep, then president of the Chicago & Northwestern Railroad, sent for Flower to take care of his many investments. Keep, who was his brother-in-law, had numerous financial interests, and being in failing health entrusted to Flower the care of his big properties. Flower's handling of Keep's interests was eminently successful and, during his management, while Keep was alive, the property substantially increased in value. It was here that Flower's great interest in Wall Street and its ramifications was created and, in 1870, he formed the firm of Benedict, Flower & Co., which two years after was dissolved. A short time later, he organized the banking firm of Flower & Co., which was a power in the Street until the time of his death.

Who or what brought Flower into politics is not known. But in the early 1870s Flower was associated with Samuel J. Tilden to expose and smash "Boss" Tweed and his infamous political ring in New York. He was chosen in 1877 to be chairman of the Democratic State Committee and, in 1881, he defeated William Waldorf Astor for Congress after an exciting campaign. This election was a special one to fill a vacancy caused by the resignation of Levi P. Morton, who had been appointed by President Cleveland as United States minister to France. Flower's popularity was demonstrated by the fact that he was elected by a majority of 3,100, whereas Morton, a Republican, had secured the place in the last previous election by more than 7,000 votes.

In 1882 Flower was a candidate for governor of New York state, but was beaten by Cleveland. In 1886 he was president of the New York Electric Subway Commission and in the Democratic

Flower became governor of New York in 1891, serving for four years.

National Convention of 1888 he was mentioned as an available presidential nominee. He had a large following, including a delegation from New York State, but Cleveland was renominated. Flower came close to getting the highest honor in the land, which is convincing proof of the man's integrity.

From then on, Flower's association with New York State politics was close. He was representative from the 12th district in the Fifty-first Congress, and was re-elected to the Fifty-second Congress. Flower became governor of New York in 1891, serving for four years.

Although Flower was a politician, one gets an insight into the broad humanity of the man in the following incident:

There was a cholera epidemic in the late summer of 1892 in New York and passengers from Europe were quarantined down the Bay. Flower bought, with his own money, the Fire Island Hotel in the name of the state and ordered the passengers be sent there. Long Islanders secured an injunction to prevent the immigrants landing. Fearing that the incident might lead to controversy, which would affect the Governor's political future, a member of his staff suggested that he manage the affair so that the Governor would not lose a vote. Flower reported that he didn't care a profanely small amount for the votes, but he was going to "get those unfortunate people ashore and comfortable."

He did. He sent the passengers ashore and ordered the militia to arrest them for violating the injunction, but to confine them in a comfortable hotel.

Flower's big and spectacular operations in Wall Street began after he had served a term as governor and returned to the bank- *He believed in the* ing firm of Flower & Co. Flower *future of New York City.* preached optimism. He believed in his state. He believed in the future of New York City, and when he came back from the gubernatorial chair, he brought with him a tremendous following. Flower had made many friends, who would follow him blindly in all his fortunes. Naturally, having been in high political office, he brought considerable prestige and this attracted attention to him. Although Flower's party loyalty (he was always a Democrat) had never been questioned, he had, during the term at the capital, made friends alike of Republicans and Democrats and many of these were traders in the market. Naturally when Flower came to be active again in the Street, they followed him.

Moreover, Flower had always been friendly with and had had the confidence of many of the larger capitalists of New York and his first big ventures in the Street were in Federal Steel, Rock Island, and People's Gas. Under Flower's leadership, these securities developed great activity and showed big increases in market value. This in itself was sufficient to attract investors and traders from all parts of the country to the Flower stocks and when Flower started the famous buying movement in Brooklyn Rapid Transit, which was one of the most remarkable advances the stock has ever seen, he had back of him the gigantic buying power of his followers.

When Flower first took hold of Brooklyn Rapid Transit, the stock was selling around $6 a share. Flower had become the leader of the Street. He was neither a dreamer nor a reckless guesser. He needed no introduction, no recommendation. He had learned the advantage of knowing public sentiment and he had that long range vision that sees business activity, better prices, better wages and cheap money. He once said (and it was his platform to the day he died), "I believe in better American security values, because I believe in our country."

Flower believed in the growth of the transportation system of New York and especially in Brooklyn Rapid Transit. The company was then broadening out, reaching into the newly developed sections around New York, and Flower could foresee the flood of nickels that was to pour into the company's coffers as New York grew. Flower began buying Brooklyn Rapid Transit and carried with him into this campaign the tremendous buying power that he had built up among his following through his success in the Street. Brooklyn Rapid Transit climbed in spite of the efforts of the professional bear element to down both Flower and his stock, and every effort they made only strengthened Flower's position. From $6 a share, in an incredibly short time, Brooklyn Rapid Transit rose to $138 a share, a gain of more than 2,000 percent.

But the rise in Brooklyn Rapid Transit carried with it the whole market and between February 1898 and February 1899, one year, the market value of the leading securities increased $5,000,000,000!

Fortunes were made almost overnight. One office boy who bought five shares of stock in October 1898 was able to make his parents a present of a $5,000 suburban home in the following spring. A packer in New York making a $200 investment had in a short time $50,000 to his credit. An umbrella maker in Boston had bought a Philadelphia Electric stock at $35 a share and sold it out at $135. His final profit was more than $100,000. A trader in Wall Street came to an acquaintance one day, asking for the loan of $100. He had been in hard luck and was in debt. Three months from the day the loan was made, it was returned and with the

The Flower market was probably the greatest constructive market ever seen. check was a note, asking that the lender call to see something unusual. It was the result of that $100. The exhibit was a batch of receipts for old bills, a deed to a $30,000 home and bank books and brokerage accounts, showing a credit balance of more than $50,000.

The big operators of the period made tremendous fortunes, but so did the smaller investor. The Flower market was probably the greatest constructive market of its kind that has ever been seen and one in which the traders small and large participated equally, according to their investments. All through this momentous era, Flower preached Americanism and confidence and the Flower market was really an adjustment of securities values to the increasing wealth of the country, which needed but the genuine optimism of Flower to set the wheels in motion.

It was unfortunate that right at the height of Flower's success he died. The story is that Mr Flower went to the country for a day's rest, ate freely of ham and radishes and washed the meal down with a generous supply of ice water. He died a few hours afterward of an attack of acute indigestion.

With the death of Flower, it was believed that values would crack. The professional bear element, scenting what the loss of leadership might mean to the market, came out from the holes in which they had been ensconced during the tremendous constructive era and attempted to break the market.

But they did not reckon with Flower's friends. Flower had with him the Rockefellers, the Vanderbilts, and the other financial powers of the Street. Moreover, Flower had made friends with the financial reporters of the city and it was quickly pointed out that the advance in stocks was based on a great deal more than Flower's operations. It was based on a development of the country. In other words, it was the catching up of securities values to the values that had been put behind the properties these securities represented.

The arguments carried conviction and with the financial giants of the Street checking the attempted raid of the bears, a severe crash in prices was averted.

Flower's personality was unique. He was a plain man, talking plain talk, having simple ideas, a part of, not apart from, the people. Henry Clews, banker and veteran of Wall Street, in his intensely interesting reminiscences of the Street, gives the following pen picture of Flower, the man:

> Roswell P. Flower, ex-governor of the state of New York, was the leader of the boom and a more picturesque figure has never been seen in Wall Street, which is saying a great deal. Mr Flower was an

individual of very plain exterior. He often used language that was noticeable more for its force and directness and emphasis, than it was for polish. He had an ambling gait and looked like a well-fed farmer. He was rarely seen without a huge quid of tobacco that almost filled the left side of his mouth. Spittoons were an essential part of the furnishings of his office. His clothing hung on his person not unlike meal sacks. His hat was rarely brushed and for days at a time, apparently, he forgot to shave. Altogether he was the last person, in appearance, who might be expected to lead in a district that is famous for its well groomed men.

His education was certainly not collegiate; doubtless all his peculiar traits the ordinary man would have judged a handicap, still they were Mr Flower's strongest aids. The lack of artificial polish gave people confidence in his statements. His limited education enabled him to think clearly along certain lines without being hampered with mental digressions, which would probably have come with a higher original mental culture.

Whatever Flower's personality may have been, whatever his peculiar characteristics, whatever his political creeds or ambitions,

People believed in the Flower stocks because they believed in Governor Flower.

he remains in the mind of Wall Street as one of its greatest constructionist forces. Flower was a creator of market values, the embodiment of optimism and confidence, a leader of the market, not a driver. The Flower market is an accurate demonstration of how united public buying, under capable leadership, can influence the market value of securities.

People believed in the Flower stocks because they believed in

Governor Flower – in his shrewdness, in his integrity, and in his ability to direct wisely and carry out the enterprises in which he was concerned. They believed in his conscience as well as in his head, and they trusted him.

THOMAS F. RYAN

Thomas F. Ryan is one of the few men who had the distinction of beating the wily, redoubtable James R. Keene in a pitched battle in the market. This, of itself, testifies to his capabilities as a stock market operator. Like Gates, reorganization and expansion are the secret of Mr Ryan's success. Forceful, persevering, but withal a great compromiser, he has been identified with some of the most interesting pages of America's financial history.

THOMAS F. RYAN

....

Fortunes acquired through operations on the constructive side of the securities market may roughly be divided into three classes: those which have been made in foreseeing adjustment of market prices to previously improved business conditions (relations of prices and values); those that have been made in the rehabilitation of fallen fortunes of promising corporations; and those of the optimists who have possessed the courage and daring to swim with the rising tide to the full extent of their resources.

Of the three groups, probably the second is the least spectacular, but of more lasting interest because of involving the creation and expansion of corporation wealth and in many cases the transmutation of ruin into affluence. Gates was of this type. So was the late J. P. Morgan, father of the present head of the famous banking house, and so also is that great figure of the traction and tobacco worlds, who has retired to his home in the Sunny South – Thomas F. Ryan.

Contemporary of William C. Whitney, P. A. B. Widener, Yerkes, Belmont, and other so-called "Lords of the Street," Ryan has been one of the big figures in the securities markets of the world for some fifty years. Some idea of Mr Ryan's capabilities as a market operator is indicated in the fight for the control in the open market of the Metropolitan Street Railways of New York, which involved a pitched battle with that greatest of all market operators of his generation, James R. Keene, and in which Mr Ryan was victorious.

Aggressive, forceful, silent, the secret of Ryan's huge fortune may be epitomized in a single word, "reorganization." His plans were masterly and in the execution of those plans, great force, carried almost to the point of ruthlessness, brought them to a successful consummation. Yet Mr Ryan had that keen, well-balanced business mind that is back of all great successes. He knew when to fight and he knew when to compromise. An exhibition of the latter attribute is shown in the sudden ending of the international tobacco war that followed the invasion of England by Mr Ryan's then recently organized tobacco organization.

World War I threatened to waste millions of dollars in ruinous competition and demoralize the whole trade. Mr Ryan went to London alone and the English interests attempted to conduct the proceedings with all the formality that is dear to the British heart. Mr Ryan's methods were characteristically American. He took the head of the British tobacco interests into a side room and on a single sheet of paper drew up an agreement satisfactory to both sides and brought instant peace to the warring camps.

Thomas F. Ryan was born in 1851 in the Blue Ridge Mountains of Virginia in Nelson County. His paternal ancestors came from the north of Ireland, while on his mother's side he is of Scottish-Irish descent. At the age of five, he lost his mother and went to live with his grandmother. His early days were spent in the shadow of the Civil War, and at the age of 15, he assumed charge of his grandmother's estate and managed it well, considering the ravages of the war. But the entire country was in a slough of despond and, two years later, Ryan gave up the attempt and went to Baltimore. He was broke, but secured a place in the dry goods store of John S. Barry, whose daughter he later married, and for two years existed on a small salary, when his employer offered him a place in a banking house which he was about to establish in New York. Here for some years young Ryan got his first financial training.

It was in 1873 that Mr Ryan was definitely established in the brokerage business and in 1884 first appeared lined up with the street railroad interests. He appears with William C. Whitney at the head of a traction company, seeking a franchise under the legislative act of that year to build a street railroad on Broadway, New York. Whitney went to Washington and Ryan formed an alliance with that remarkable group of operators in traction stocks – Widener, Elkins, and Kemble of Philadelphia – who had just come through with the successful organization of the Philadelphia Union Traction. In a political upheaval a short time later, Mr Ryan was questioned rather sharply by Roscoe Conkling regarding the methods used in getting a franchise. He is described as a fashionable young man of about 30, answering questions with good humor, making friends of the investigating committee and the reporters and even of his questioner. Mr Ryan had secured a franchise and he fought for it tooth and nail, winning out in the long run through a battle in the courts and establishing himself firmly in the traction annals of New York City.

One of Mr Ryan's biographers some years ago said it seemed

incredible that he had been associated with so many enterprises and, were a full and true account of his activities in the twenty years subsequent to 1885 written, one would get a pretty good financial history of the United States.

Although an element of Mr Ryan's success has been the forceful personality that he must have inherited from his ancestors, he

"He combines to an extraordinary degree the powers of a harmonizer with those of a fighter."

has appeared from time to time as a master of compromise and a genius of harmonization – to quote from one who made a study of him some years ago: "He combines to an extraordinary degree the powers of a harmonizer with those of a fighter. The surprising effects of his mere personal charm are constantly manifest. Notice, for example, that during his early years he held his place at once with Tammany Hall and in close alliance with Mr Whitney who was fighting Tammany tooth and nail within the ranks of the Democratic party and notice that he was able to take allies much more powerful than he, without surrendering to them the fruits of victory. That skill has never deserted him. He has also had incongruous friends and men who are naturally incorrigible enemies have worked together easily through him as a sort of mollifying medium. He has a knack for just the phrase that releases the tension in a dangerous moment."

Ryan during his early career in market affairs made many powerful friends, among whom were William R. Travers, Samuel J. Taylor, John R. Garland, John B. Trevor, and Robert L. Cutting – all large Wall Street operators of those days. When he entered the traction field, he became associated with A. J. Cassatt, Frank Thomason, and John D. Crimmins.

Whitney once said that he was the most adroit, suave, and noiseless man he had ever known.

Mr Ryan has always shunned the limelight of publicity. One of the first things the young cub financial reporter of a metropolitan newspaper learned was that "Thomas F. Ryan won't talk." Yet the magnitude of his operations in the Street and in other fields of finance have dragged him into the spotlight from time to time. One of the most conspicuous of these was the great fight in the market between the Morgan and the Whitney-Ryas interests on Consolidated Gas. He acquired the Hocking Valley Railroad, reorganized it, rehabilitated it, and sold it – at a profit naturally. He did practically the same thing with Pere Marquette. And again with the Seaboard Air Line.

The most conspicuous was the great fight between Morgan and the Whitney-Ryan interests.

In connection with the reorganization and rehabilitation of Seaboard Air Line, a phase of Mr Ryan's character – persistence – is brought strongly to the fore. It forms one of the most picturesque episodes of his career. Ryan's fight for control of the Seaboard Air Line was one of the bitterest struggles in the annals of railroad financial history. Ryan saw great possibilities for the company, but he was opposed by a group of southern interests, who were skillful enough to thwart the big men until it was firmly believed that Ryan was beaten. Although apparently withdrawn from the field, he was far from swerved in his purpose to secure control of the railroad property. He kept hammering away for years and eventually the road fell upon hard times and the interests in control were forced to pledge their stock.

A mysterious saviour had appeared, but after the management woke up, it was found that their supposed benefactor was none other than their old opponent, Thomas F. Ryan.

It took time; it took perseverance; undoubtedly it took a lot of money. But Ryan, after eight years, secured the road on practically his own terms.

One other great reorganization stands out in Mr Ryan's career, and one which brought him very much into the public eye. This was the purchase of the control of the Equitable Life Insurance Co. after the tremendous Hyde sensation. Two years after he acquired the controlling interest in the big insurance company, he said that the controlling factor in the purchase was the desire to do a public service, to do a constructive service into which the element of money making did not enter at all. It is improbable, however, that Ryan did not make money out of his acquisition of the control of the Equitable company, as he made money in his other reorganizations and consolidations, whether railroad or industrial corporations.

The wealth of Thomas F. Ryan is numbered among the large fortunes of the country. But it is the fortune that ought to accrue to a man of Ryan's type that has created values, for the career of Mr Ryan is punctuated with the organization, reorganization, and expansion of corporations that now occupy a permanent place in the financial fabric of the country. His creed has apparently been to make two dollars grow where one grew before and to the man who can thus create, there is due a substantial share of the product of his fertile and forceful mind.

Those enterprises with which Mr Ryan has been identified in a large way have been successful. They have been successful for stockholders, in that the creative genius of Ryan consequent to acquiring their control was quickly reflected in improved securities prices. The battle for control were fought in the arena of

Mr Ryan fought battles with the greatest masters of stock market operations of his generation.

the Street and the success with which Mr Ryan fought those battles and which brought him in conflict with the greatest masters of stock market operations of his generation is sufficient tribute to his genius.

Nearly thirty years ago it was said of Mr Ryan, "The success of his business career, culminating in a fortune of several millions, is obviously due to his enormous will power, unrelenting perseverance and breadth of mental vision. Not only has his strict integrity won the esteem of all with whom he has been associated, but as an executive railroad and corporation financier he is probably without a superior today in the United States."

And although Mr Ryan has practically retired from the Street, the thoughts expressed in that appreciation of nearly three decades ago hold true today.

Little has been heard of Mr Ryan in recent years, but one of his sons has been very much in the public eye, the achievements of whom is a story in itself. The career of Allan A. Ryan suggests that his father, the subject of this sketch, has decided that his son shall carve his own destiny. It has been stated authoritatively that he has never had any hand in his son's financial affairs.

In 1917, Mr Ryan offered 2,000 acres of his Virginia farm to the Government for a cavalry remount and training station. On that occasion he was combatting the charge that our capitalistic economic system tends only to avarice and corruption. He said, "If the element of seeking distinction above his fellows were eliminated from the nature of man, most men would be deprived of their motive for doing great things. After they have acquired a competency, it is for distinction that most men strive, rather than for money."

Yet it did not apply to himself. He has never sought distinction. He has no political ambitions. One who saw him at the time of his offer of a part of his farm said:

Mr Ryan's personal history is more or less written in his appearance. Some observers call him handsome, others distinguished looking; I should not apply either term to him, except in a very restricted sense. I should describe him, rather, as a noticeable man. His powerful frame and his square face, his cleft chin, and the outward arch of his eyebrows, would make him that. His Irish origin is obvious to the first glance; almost or quite as certain as his country upbringing and the fact that he had to make his own way in life and has made it as he set out to do.

The conventional perfection of his attire or the environment we associate with riches, serve to obscure the signs with which nature has stamped him. His personality is forceful rather than attractive, like the steel bar which is hard to touch and resonant in response to a blow, but bends without cracking under the influence of heat. You can see that he is naturally a brilliant man as to anything which concerns himself and even when, in the company of old friends, he has grown genial, you never expect to see his geniality melt into conventional intimacy. So when he gets ready to tell the world the full meaning of his latest act and not before that, we shall know – just as much as he is willing that we should.

Mr Ryan has been for some years at his home in Oak Ridge in Nelson County, Virginia, practically on the spot where he was born. Here he raises cattle and horses and swaps stories with his neighbors, who call him "Tom." He has a fine old mansion on Fifth Avenue, near Washington Square, and it is a home in the strictest sense of the word.

Mr Ryan's operations in the market have never savored of the spectacular. When he was a young man, it was said of him that, "His right hand never knew what his left was doing." But he has been a powerful uplifting force in certain classes of securities, one of those great builders of financial America, seeking the tools of Wall Street to aid in the construction and establishment of a new era and a new high standard in corporation history of the United States. And although apparently withdrawn from the Street, he is still a commanding figure and a director of the destinies of many important financial structures.

HENRY H. ROGERS

To Henry Rogers may be attributed the rise of
Standard Oil as a world financial power. Leader of the
mass millions of the huge organization, the magnitude
of his operations in the market made financial history.
Despotic, fiery, a natural leader, his friendship with
Mark Twain and the daily interruption to the internal
financial battle for a few minutes (to telephone my
mother), established him as a personality that has left
a permanent record in the annals of Wall Street.

HENRY H. ROGERS

....

All financial roads at some point in their course, bend through Wall Street and the stock market. Many roads end there.

Many begin at that most interesting spot and lead to the four corners of the earth. Likewise to some men operations in the stock market are but the means to an end. To some it is the be-all and end-all of success, while still others are drawn unwillingly to the magnet, sometimes for their own good, sometimes otherwise.

It was inevitable that the fortunes of Standard Oil as it grew into a financial power and as employment for its accumulation of *All financial roads bend* wealth was sought, should be bound *through Wall Street and* up in some measure with important *the stock market.* stock market operations, as they undoubtedly still are and always will be.

It was inevitable, also, that the master mind of the Standard Oil organization, the mind that lifted Standard Oil out of the role as a mere oil producer, marketer, and refiner into a world financial power, should be the directing force of some of the biggest operations in the market.

Thus does Henry H. Rogers appear in the role of a stock market operator. Rogers controlled the purse strings of the Standard Oil money bag during his lifetime, and the man who controls the purse strings is the power that makes prices move in the security markets of the world.

Henry H. Rogers entered the employ of the Standard Oil Co. when it was merely an oil business. At Rogers's death, some 40 years later, the organization was the greatest financial power in the United States. For Rogers was the leader, in shining armor, of the Standard Oil fortunes. His was the great driving force that built the imposing structure of millions, the seed planter of Standard Oil dollars in every corner of the world, from which the Standard Oil *He was the man of iron, the driving dynamo energized by the Rockefeller money.* organization and John D. Rockefeller have reaped gigantic harvests. It was Rogers who carried Standard Oil into copper; Rogers who stood shoulder to shoulder with the elder Morgan in the great steel combine; Rogers who sent Standard Oil money into hundreds of enterprises; Rogers, one of the giant financial minds of the world and without which the Standard Oil organization might still be an oil business – a large one, it is true – but still an oil business.

Whatever the capabilities of the Rockefellers, their attainments must pale before the tremendous ability and personality of Henry H. Rogers. He was the man of iron in the organization, the driving dynamo energized by the Rockefeller money.

In appearance, Rogers was everything that one might imagine in a man capable of directing the fortunes of Standard Oil. But one who knew him intimately, who had worked cheek-by-jowl with him for many years, painted the following word picture, which is considered unusually accurate:

> At sixty-five, Henry H. Rogers is probably one of the most distinguished looking men of the time; tall and straight and as well

proportioned and supple as one of the beautiful American elms which line the streets of his native town. All able men have some of God's indelible imprints of greatness. When he walks the active swing of his figure expresses power – realized, confident power. When at rest or inaction, his square jaw tells of fighting power, bull-dog hold-on, never-let-go, fighting power and his high forehead of intellectual, mightily intellectual power and they are reinforced with cheekbones and nose, which suggest that this fighting power has in it something of the ruthlessness of the North American Indian.

His eyes, however, are the crowning characteristic of the man's physical makeup. One must see Mr Rogers's eyes in action and in repose to half appreciate their wonders. I can only say that they are red, blue and black, brown, gray, and green; I have seen them when they were so restfully blue that I would think they never could be anything but a part of those skies that come with the August and September afternoons when the bees hum and the locusts drone, blent with the smell of new mown hay to help spell the word, "rest." I have seen them so green that within their depths, I was almost sure the fish were lazily resting in the shadows of those sea plants which grow only on the ocean's bottom; and I have seen them as black as that thunder cloud, which makes us wonder, "Is he angry?" And then again I have watched them when they were of the fiery red and that glinting yellow, which one sees only when at night the doors of a great roaring furnace are opened.

There is such a kindly goodwill in these eyes when they are at rest that the man does not live who would not consider himself favored to be allowed to turn over to Henry H. Rogers his pocket-book without receiving a receipt. They are the eyes of a man you would name in your will to care for your wife's and children's welfare.

H. H. Rogers was a product of New England. He was born at Fairhaven, Mass., and we first hear of him doing odd chores for the neighbors in Fairhaven, earning an average of fifty cents a week. His ability as an organizer was apparent at an early age, when he established a news route of forty-seven subscribers for the *New Bedford Standard* and in one week doubled the number. He then worked in a grocery store and with Charles Ellis, a schoolfellow, went to the Pennsylvania oil fields to make his fortune. Each of them had about $200 and the two entered the refining business in a small way.

Later one finds him associated with Charles Pratt, who had become a refiner of petroleum on Long Island. In 1872 the Pratt company, one of the Standard's most formidable competitors, was

The big brain, the big body, the head of Standard Oil is Henry H. Rogers. absorbed by the Standard Oil interests and Henry H. Rogers came to the notice of the Rockefellers. From this point on, he became an ever increasing factor in Standard Oil affairs, which eventually led to dominance of the entire Standard Oil organization. To quote again from his former associate:

"John D. Rockefeller may have more money, more actual dollars, than Henry H. Rogers or all other members of the Standard Oil family, and in the early history of Standard Oil may have been looked up to as the big gun by his partners, and allowed to take the hugest hunks of the profits, and may have so handled and judiciously invested these as to be at the beginning of the twentieth century the richest man on earth, but none of these things alters the fact that the big brain, the big body, the head of Standard Oil is Henry H. Rogers."

If Rogers was a dictator in the affairs of the Standard Oil Co., he was equally a dictator in such big market operations as were conducted in association with the leading financiers of the Street. He brooked no interference. He might use one or a dozen of the biggest market operators, but they were always acting under the direction of Henry H. Rogers, when they were using Standard Oil money. How many tremendous market coups attributed to the various clever and daring men of his time were really planned in the fertile brain of Henry H. Rogers will probably never be known. Failure was not in his dictionary and woe to the individual who attempted to interfere with his plans. Many times, big men who were associated with him in market operations resented being told what to do by H. H. Rogers. They never "resented it" twice.

For Rogers was a dictator. He could afford to be. He had the greatest aggregation of millions back of him, and when he went into the market those millions lashed it to fury. It was only in matters of very great moment that Rogers undertook to consult the Rockefellers, William and John. For the most part, he was piloting the great organization alone and the Rockefellers were supremely content with Henry H. Rogers's direction.

Naturally, being in a position to create and destroy market values, Rogers was besieged with requests for "tips" on the market. Every market operator must at some time lay down a policy regarding his friends. Either he must put a padlock on his mouth or else conceal his real operations by talking about all the stocks except the one in which he is vitally interested. It is evident from those who knew Mr Rogers that he adopted the latter method. He would talk of the possibilities of so-called "Standard Oil stocks," but it is chronicled that the tips went wrong more often than they went right and after a time there were few who cared to ask Henry H. Rogers's advice regarding any of the securities in which he was supposed to be interested, which was probably just what Rogers wanted.

It was Rogers who gave to America the greatest copper producing organization of its kind today, Anaconda. The consolidation of the properties that go to make up the great Anaconda organization is a stormy page of financial history. But today the great vision of Rogers is a reality. It has been men like Rogers and the elder Morgan that have set new high standards to the country's business.

Morgan, with his tremendous foresight, his long range vision of the country's development that could conceive a time when billion-dollar corporations should be commonplace, Morgan, the creator of the United States Steel Corporation, a world power in itself.

Rogers with his far-seeing vision of America dominant in the copper industry of the world, with belief in the future of Butte, belief sufficient to justify backing a consolidation of the more important properties of the camp into the splendid thing that Anaconda has become today. The consolidation and introduction to the public of that great group of mines through the medium of the market, needed a personality of the character of Henry H.

Rogers. And the entrance of Standard Oil into the copper industry may be said to have marked the beginning of the rise of the United States to supremacy in the world's production of red metal.

One of the most beautiful things in Henry H. Rogers's life, the offsetting feature to this despotic, domineering side of his nature, was his devotion to his mother. A few years before he died, Mr Rogers said:

"Up to a very few years ago, I went to my mother with all my joys and all my woes just as I had when a boy."

Once a week in Fairhaven, for which Mr Rogers did a great deal, he drove to the grave of that mother he loved. When she was alive, he was connected with a long distance telephone and every morning in his New York office, at precisely 11 o'clock, in the very midst of his battles of millions, he would call a truce for a few minutes, "to telephone my mother."

It was one of the finest sides of his character. It has been said of him that he was one of the most charming and lovable beings, a man whom any man or woman would be proud to have for a brother, a man any mother or father would give thanks to have for a son, a man whom any woman would be happy to know as her husband, a man whom any boy or girl should rejoice to call father.

This is the other side of the medal, the human side of the fiery, impetuous dictator to the many kings of Wall Street. His enemies say he never forgot an injury; his friends know that he never forgot a kindness. He never said an unkind word, even of his worst enemies and he never asked for any consideration.

A man who made strong friends of such men as Mark Twain, Dr. Robert Collier, Thomas B. Reid, and Booker T. Washington, must have had something besides hard cash to do it with. Twice a week for some ten years, Mr Rogers stopped at Mark Twain's house on Fifth Avenue on his way down to business to inquire how his old friend was. And one night every week, when he was in town, Mark went up to Rogers's home to spend the evening playing cards and talking.

In 1904 an enterprise very dear to Mr Rogers's heart was launched. This was at first the Tidewater Railway Co., afterwards to be known as the Virginian Railway. Mr Rogers started to build a great railroad. He summoned the aid of the ablest engineers to point out the proposed line. The completed system went into operation on July 1, 1909. The Virginian Railway operates 504 miles of main track and the Virginian Terminal Railway, at Sewall's Point, Virginia, one of the finest coal loading ports in existence. Its mile costs are said to be the lowest in the United States. It traverses a region whose coal reserves are estimated at 20,100,000,000 tons.

Mr Rogers lived long enough to see the first train run over the road. He realized, several years before his sudden demise, that he was marked for quick passing, and he began to unload some of his heavy responsibilities upon the shoulders of his son, H. H., Jr. Among these responsibilities was a share in the management of the Standard Oil pipe lines. Another was a directorship in Amalgamated Copper, now Anaconda. A third, the most sentimental of all, was a directorship in the Virginian Railway. This last was one of the great projects of Mr Rogers's life. It is said that Mr Rogers remarked, not long before his death, that some of the pangs of his passing were alleviated by the realization that he had a worthy son to perpetuate his name.

JESSE L. LIVERMORE

*Today he stands as the greatest of the stock market
operators. Upon him has fallen the mantle of James R.
Keene, master of the Street in a former generation.
But those who know something of the methods of
Livermore say that he is greater than any of his
predecessors. His accomplishments in the Street to
date read like a page of fiction, and at forty-five, he is
famous. What will the next few years bring him?*

JESSE L. LIVERMORE

Imagine a severely plain, small office, a small flat-top desk, two chairs, a Spartan-like severity of furnishings; not even a scrap of paper in sight. The hour is 10:30. By the side of the ticker stands a tall, well-built man, straight as an arrow; a man in the pink of physical condition; a man 45 years old, with an immobile face, standing motionless watching the unreeling of the white tape, denoting the ebb and flow of battle in the markets; a man with *He is the veteran of a hundred or more Wall Street battles.* keen, gray-blue eyes, impervious to everything in the world except that little white ribbon with its mysterious signs and figures, pouring out from under the glass dome. Occasionally he will walk over into a soundproof telephone booth. Sometimes a clerk will come in to speak to him. He nods or shakes his head. No lines appear on his face, although he is the veteran of a hundred or more Wall Street battles.

His mind is working with perfect precision, but his pulse fails to register one beat less or one beat more, as the tape unfolds its story, which may increase or diminish the fortunes of this man by hundreds of thousands of dollars.

One can imagine almost the figures on the tape crawling through his fingers to his arms and up into that mind that has proven one of the greatest Wall Street has ever known and as you see him in his workshop, it would appear that all the human life

blood had been drained from him and in its place had been sub-
stituted the white ticker tape.

Imagine again, a few hours later when the tape begins printing
the closing prices. There is no relaxation of tension, because there
has been no tension. The man moves away from the ticker as one

Considered head and moves away from the study of an inter-
shoulders above any of esting piece of machinery when it stops.
the stock market The day's work is over and you have
operators in Wall Street. before you a very human character, a
man of infinitely charming personality, a man who still looks
boyish in spite of his years, a man who is considered head and
shoulders above any of the stock market operators that have yet
appeared in Wall Street – Jesse L. Livermore.

It must be a constant source of amusement to Mr Livermore to
read what the many financial scribes of the newspapers say about
him. According to these veracious gentlemen, practically every
major market move of recent years has been ascribed to
Livermore. He is reputed to have had a finger in every rise and fall
that has been hitherto unexplained. The market goes up.
"Livermore is buying." The market goes down. "Livermore is
raiding it." It has been proven more than once that at the time a
tremendous bear drive was taking place and which depression
was accredited to Livermore's operations, he has been quietly
enjoying himself in some out-of-the-way place, probably out on
the broad Atlantic, fishing, or watching a yacht race, or otherwise
recuperating from the daily five-hour concentration. There is no
doubt but that Livermore has swayed portions of the market from

time to time, but to ascribe some of the gigantic moves of the whole list to Livermore activity is the height of absurdity.*

As a matter of fact, Livermore's operations have been running with the tide, instead of endeavoring to create it. He is a power in the market, one to be seriously reckoned with, as many of the other operators in Wall Street know. But general market movements are created, not by individuals, but by conditions, aided by great consolidations of moneyed forces.

Livermore started with nothing. Today he is rich. And it has all come from operations in the market. There are, no doubt, a million people in the United States – probably ten million – who

The success of Livermore is based first on an ability to read the tape.

would like to ask Mr Livermore just one question: "How did you do it?" There are many who have asked him that question and until recently they have received no response. Livermore, however, in the recent year or so has been inclined to be more talkative and one is beginning to gain an insight into the secrets of his success.

At the foundation of it all is sheer common sense.

The success of Livermore is based first on an ability to read the tape. He has given years of study to it – in fact, practically ever since he was a board boy in a Boston brokerage house. Second, a study of national and world conditions that affect markets. Third,

Editor's note:
* On October 24, 1929 the author could add a ditto to this statement here for, on that date, "Black Thursday," when the New York Stock Exchange saw its greatest fall percentagewise for one day, the cry went up, "Livermore's selling." He wasn't.

· 99 ·

an analysis of market cycles. In connection with the last, is told an interesting story regarding Livermore in his early days. One of the traders in a commission house where Livermore conducted his

"But it's a bull market." operations had bought a security that
All he would answer had advanced substantially. He was
was, "It's a bull advised that the stock had advanced far
market." enough and it was suggested that he

take his profits. He demurred. "But it's a bull market," he said. He was advised that a reaction ought to set in and he might be able to buy in cheaper. He refused to lose his market position. All he would answer was, "It's a bull market."

It is said that Livermore gained from this conversation one of the greatest secrets of his success. He realized that in a bull market one must be a consistent bull. The big profits are made not in attempting to catch each little backing and filling in the market, but in the long constructive period, covering a whole phase of the cycle. It is something that any investor may well paste in his hat.

Like many other men who have made Wall Street history, Jesse Livermore is a product of New England. He was born at Shrewsbury, Mass., and spent his early years in Worcester. At fourteen, he secured his first position as a board boy with a Boston brokerage house.

At first it was merely a job of changing figures on a board. He then became interested as to why the figures changed. Here began Livermore's life study of the tape. His early ventures in the market were successful. From an initial transaction in which he made a profit of about $3, his operations grew until he was, in the parlance of the Street, able to "swing a line." Some unusually successful operations gained him the sobriguet of "kid plunger."

Don't imagine Livermore has always been successful. It is by our mistakes that we grow in capability and Livermore was no exception. His continued success led him to broaden his operations more and more until he was getting into fields that were too large for his immature experience. The result was he went broke. Recognizing instantly that he lacked some of the elements that make for permanent success, he applied himself to the closer study of markets and conditions – to more intensive study of the tape. He discovered new things. His vision expanded and it was not long before he was on the high road again toward fortune.

Again as late as 1914, he was "down and out" only to come back in a spectacular manner and make more money than he had ever made before.

As one talks to Mr Livermore, one begins to get some perception of the quality of that mind that has made him the best tape reader and the greatest stock market operator alive. He can recall *He has the same type of* to the tiniest detail the exact number *mind as the late James* of shares and the prices of stocks *R. Keene.* bought and sold twenty years ago. He has the type of mind of a great chess player, with every possible "position" as the tape registers it in his mind and the answering play. He remembers quotations and fluctuations indefinitely. He can tell what a stock sold at when he became bullish or bearish on it more than a decade ago. He has the same type of mind as the late James R. Keene, only with a still finer edge, ground to sharpness on the ever moving ticker tape.

Moreover, he has another attribute that Keene had – the sense of "hunch." There is that same keen, intuitive perception that led Keene to do what would seem to be almost unreasonable and to fly in the face of what appeared to be sound reasoning and good judgment.

Livermore does the same thing. He will suddenly abandon what appears to be a strong market position and do nothing for several days, later to discover that he had avoided an ingenious trap.

What tells him? He cannot answer you. Perhaps even in his subconscious mind the rolling tape registers and produces caution without his conscious knowledge. Perhaps out of his constant study of world conditions, a single quotation will react on his mind as a chemist, pouring one white fluid from a test tube into another test tube filled with the same colored fluid, will produce a scarlet combination – a danger sign that demands instant action without reasoning. This subtle force is said to be one of Livermore's most powerful influences.

Gould used the market as a means of securing control of corporations; Vanderbilt was an investor; Morgan was a banker; Hill was a successful operator in the stocks in which he was interested; Harriman was a good trader, but also used the Street as a means to secure control of railroads; Keene, the master mind of his generation, was usually working in the interests of some of the great financiers. Not so Livermore. Up to within a short time ago, one stock was as good as another to him. Cotton, grain, and other commodities all were vehicles for Livermore's money making. It may be said that practically every active security on the list has been affected at one time or another, in one way or another, by Livermore's operations.

Recently, however, Livermore, recognized as a master operator in securities, is assuming the position occupied by James R. Keene. He is no longer the freelance of the markets. He is operating little today with his own money. It is reported from time to time that Livermore is active in the market, but he is probably in these operations, serving some of the greatest financial powers of the country who have big coups in the Street in process.

Thus Livermore today is a more powerful force than he has ever

Then he should find out why he is going to buy it.

been. His operations, because of the greater financial strength back of him, are broadened. He no longer gathers the crumbs from Wall Street's table – he carves the main course.

In May 1922, Livermore, visiting his father and mother on their sixtieth wedding anniversary, gave some idea of the reasoning that makes him buy securities. He said:

Now what is the best thing for the average man to do? The thing for him to do is say to himself, "I am going to buy such-and-such a stock." Then he should find out *why* he is going to buy it.

Let him have a good reason. Here's an example: A short time ago there were rumors that Studebaker was to pay a big dividend. So the stock went up. I had been watching Studebaker. The time came for the dividend and the directors declared one less than was expected. What did I do? Did I sell Studebaker short? I did not. I let the other fellow do that. The other fellow argued if the dividend wasn't as big as it was expected to be, then Studebaker would drop. But I knew better than that. I knew that Studebaker could pay the big dividend if it wished, and just because it didn't was no reason for the stock to go down. Its earnings warranted it. It would have to pay it sooner or later. So I bought Studebaker when the other fellow wanted to sell it – a very good time to buy. Fellows thought I was crazy but [and he smiled] I wasn't. I had studied that stock; that is why I was able to make money on it. A man with enough money can go into the stock market any day and make money.

Many successful bear operations have been falsely credited to Livermore, and the breaking of the long silence shows that his big successes have been on the constructive side of the market. Livermore made his first fortune in the boom of 1901. In the long, lean period just prior to the war Livermore's fortune dwindled away to nothing and he went into bankruptcy for about $2,000,000.

"I had studied that stock; that is why I was able to make money on it."

Two years later in the big war market, he is accredited with being on the constructive side and having paid the entire debt, reestablished his credit, and accumulated for himself some $3,500,000 additional.

In 1921 he became more talkative, and expressed the opinion that the market was going into a period of prosperity, that there would be a big recovery in securities values, and openly admitted he was on the constructive side of the market. His operations in this constructive period are believed to have netted him a huge fortune.

That is Livermore's method. He watches the market cycle.

In the summer of 1922 he visited the New York Curb Market. It was a surprise to the Street, who immediately began crediting him with shifting the scene of his operations. Instantly a dozen or

That is Livermore's method. He watches the market cycle

more stocks on the junior market were reported under accumulation by him. The reports were probably incorrect. But it may be that Livermore was looking over the field. His operations are so broad that no one may tell whether he is operating in a one-dollar or a hundred-dollar stock, and there is a strong suspicion that Livermore has had a finger in more than one of the major moves in the Curb market – and may have more.

How far will he go? He is still a young man. He has probably one of the greatest minds for stock market operations that has ever been seen. He has intensive training of years to guide him. He has courage and is as good a loser as he is a winner. He loves his work. With these things he can conquer. He will probably be in some of the biggest financial developments of the future. He will probably grow into an ever-increasing factor in the securities market.

RUSSELL SAGE

*Like Gould, long his partner in market operations,
Russell Sage stands among the empire-builders.
Sage knew the power of ready money. His thrift and
little economies, his caution and conservatism were by-
words of the Street in a former generation. He was one
of the powers of that phase of the market that made
America.*

RUSSELL SAGE

M any stories of success in stock market operations have each a link that forms a continuous chain – boldness. Fortunes are made by courage, that ability, as Mr Kipling so well puts it, to "make one heap of all your winnings, and risk it on one turn of pitch and toss," the ability to venture but not too far, the ability to fight a losing battle – and turn the tide into a victory. The Street

Russell Sage stands out in vivid contrast to the bold knights of Wall Street fortunes.

has few ultra cautious, ultra-conservative figures and, for that reason, Russell Sage, cautious, conservative, and what the Street would term today as a "sure thing player," stands out in vivid contrast to the bold knights of Wall Street fortunes. Sage the parsimonious, Sage the shabby, Sage who squeezed a dollar until the eagle screamed – all these stories have somewhat befogged the public mind to Sage, the empire-builder –⸱the real Sage.

A magnificent train leaves Chicago every evening and runs at record breaking speed and almost in a straight line to San Francisco. It is a product of modern civilization. Yet it was Russell Sage with Jay Gould who laid the foundations for this triumph of transportation in the creation of the Union Pacific Railroad. Few realize that Russell Sage played a large part in the construction of 5,000 miles of American railroads, or that he played an important part in the construction of the telegraph and telephone lines of this country, utilizing the stock market merely as a means to the end.

Sage built up a tremendous fortune. It was not, as many suppose, piled up dollar by dollar, but by some of the most spectacular market operations, chiefly in association with Jay Gould, the result of which was the giving to the American public of a great part of its railway transportation system. What did it matter if he accumulated a fortune valued somewhere between $75,000,000 and $100,000,000? He left a heritage worth many times this sum to the country.

To Russell Sage money was a commodity. He looked on it as something to buy cheap and sell dear. When money was scarce, Sage hoarded cash – he kept the largest cash balance of any of the big financiers of his time – and when money was dear, the Street found him a ready lender – at his own price. They say he often got 60% a month. Sage's position in this respect gained him the title of "Uncle" Russell. To the Street, Sage was always sitting under the sign of the three golden balls, hence the term, "Uncle." And not all of those who brought pledges to "Uncle" Russell's office redeemed them. The result was that Sage secured for himself some tremendous bargains and was often drawn into the active affairs of the Street unwillingly. This, of course, was in his later life and after he had accumulated his millions. But he was a tremendous force in market affairs, although he was still "playing safe." He took few chances and only one reverse is credited to him in his sensational career.

Let us for a moment see him as he was about ten years before he died, with the eyes of one of his biographers.

Mr Sage is tall and spare, with heavy eyebrows and keen, blue eyes, which are often lighted with a sense of humor. He wears no beard. He is genial in manner, prompt and decided in action, clear headed, sagacious and in speech reticent. One of his peculiarities, the plainness of his attire, has prompted harmless merriment at his expense among the men of Wall Street. Wall Street brokers are proverbially the best dressed men in the city, but Mr Sage looks more like a quiet farmer; and this entire lack of display has led several attempts by bunco men to beguile him. The surprise of these gentlemen on discovering the identity of their illustrious victim has afforded Mr Sage much entertainment and has been frequently paralleled by the sensations of rivals in Wall Street, after an attempt to engineer a speculation to Mr Sage's disadvantage and upon being confronted by the results of their attempt.

Russell Sage's life covers the period of the growth of America from a group of struggling colonies to a world power. He was born in 1816 in Troy, N.Y. and was brought up on a farm. His education was limited to the public schools of the time and his early environment was that of poverty. It is a long way back, but rumor has it that in his early years, while a clerk in his father's grocery store in Troy, he showed those characteristics of saving and self-denial which existed until the end of his life. Gossip also has it that young Sage was keen at swapping. He was sharp and early developed that sense of a good bargain, which he never lost. Sage was always looking for bargains and it was this bargain hunting quality that formed the basis of his huge fortune. By the time he was 25, Sage had accumulated $75,000, a large sum for the times. Politics attracted him and he was at one time alderman of Troy and treasurer of Rensselaer County. It was while a public official that Sage accomplished his first transaction in railroads, buying a small railroad line and selling it later to the New York Central consolidation at a substantial profit. It was in this transaction that Sage made his first million.

Sage, aiding in the election of Zachary Taylor, "Old Rough and Ready," transferred his political activities to Washington and it looked for a time as though Sage was on the way to become famous as a political leader. He was nominated to Congress and served on the Ways and Means Committee but declined a second term and, in 1861, came to Wall Street.

Jay Gould and Russell Sage first met at a railroad station in *They were perfectly* Troy, while the former was on a visit *matched, Sage the* in the interest of the Rutland & *cautious, Gould the* Washington Railroad. This acquain- *daring.* tance developed and it was probably Gould who brought Sage to Wall Street.

They were perfectly matched, a complement to each other. Sage the cautious, Gould the daring. They were in partnership in some of the biggest railroad coups ever executed in the market and in these transactions both amassed a fortune. Railroads that through ill-management had nearly reached the bankruptcy stage suddenly turned up in the control of Sage and Gould and it was usually Sage's money that paid for them.

Sage supplied the sinews of the war that Gould directed. Road after road was taken hold of by these two powerful forces and built from nothing into an important link in the country's transportation system. Practically every operation of magnitude in which Gould was interested was shared by Sage. Sage was the man with the long purse and Gould the man with the long head. The combination was invincible and more than one of their opponents felt the weight of Sage's money power, a force they could not combat. For Sage knew the effect of the concentration of the force of money at a time when the other fellows were short of it.

In 1872 Mr Sage originated the sale of privileges, a phase of the securities market that is little known to the public, because it is *"Puts" and "calls"* more or less a part of the professional *formed a big part of Mr* side of the business of Wall Street and *Sage's business.* transactions generally take place between the traders on the floor of the exchange. "Puts" and "calls" formed a big part of Mr Sage's business between 1872 and 1884. A "call" represents an agreement whereby, within a stated period, the seller agrees to deliver to the purchaser a certain number of shares at an agreed price, the purchaser paying a premium for the privilege. A "put" is an agreement on the part of the purchaser to buy a certain number of shares at an agreed price, within a specified time.

Thus if a trader believes the market is going up five to ten points within 30 days, he will endeavor to buy a "call" at a point or two above the ruling price, and when the market has advanced, call the stock and sell at the advanced figure.

On the other hand a trader who believes the market is about to decline will endeavor to make a contract for the sale of stock a point or two below the market, borrow the stock, make his delivery and then when the reaction comes, buy the stock at the lowest figure in the market and return to the borrower.

Mr Sage made a great deal of money in privileges but the failure of a financial interest in New York in 1884 cost him about $7,000,000 and he discontinued the operations. Mr Sage's little economies and the fact that, although he had amassed millions, the

It was Sage with Gould who furnished New York City with its elevated railroad.

individual dollar was just as precious as it was in his youth are shown in the fact that he retained the directorship of many corporations, attending every directors' meeting. It was not so much, according to gossip, that he was interested in the affairs of the corporation, but the fact that the directors usually received a fee for their attendance – customarily a $20 gold piece.

Sage was officially identified with some 27 corporations and over 40 railroads and some say that his income from director's fees alone took care of his meager personal expenses.

It was Sage with Gould who furnished New York City with its first adequate transportation system, the elevated railroad. It is very much in use and very much needed, in spite of the construction of huge subways in the past few years, so that it may be said that Russell Sage was a big factor in fostering the growth of New York City, because of the fact that the shape of the city demanded rapid transit if it were to grow and prosper.

Among the companies with which Mr Sage was identified were Chicago, Milwaukee & St Paul; Missouri Pacific, Union Pacific, Wabash and Pacific Mail Steamship Co. He was also during his lifetime a director of the Importers & Traders National Bank, Mercantile Trust Co., Western Union Telegraph Co., New York Bank Note Co., Standard Gas Light Co., and many others.

Among Mr Sage's admirable traits was that of being an agreeable conversationalist. He generally talked in a low gentle voice and emphasized the point of his conversation with impressive gestures. His chief recreation was with his dumb pets, notably his horses, to whom he talked as if they were human. He had no generous vices, was a model husband, owned no yacht, played no races, though he loved a fast horse and he lived a life of steady work until his ninetieth year. Although the newspapers used to love to make fun of his economies and his frugal lunch – which it was said often was three apples and a glass of water – it was learned after his death that he had been quite charitable, giving secretly and judiciously. One of his contemporaries a couple of years after he died said of him:

> The lesson in economy, of both time and money, furnished by Russell Sage, should not pass unheeded in these days of lavish expenditure and time-wasting pleasures, for economy is the foundation of the fortune of a self-made man, starting without a dollar. He must save in order to amass any capital whatever, and he should economize his time as well as his money, for time is money.
>
> The man who spends all he earns never becomes independently well off, never lays the foundation of a fortune.
>
> Russell Sage began life in extreme poverty, and earned his own living, from early boyhood. He was entirely the architect of his own fortune, and died at ninety, leaving seventy millions of dollars, more or less. If he had not been thrifty, persevering and patient, as

well as untiringly industrious, and a model of punctuality in attending to business, and also quick to see and avail himself of opportunities for money making, he would never have accumulated great wealth.

Moreover, he was very temperate, abstemious, and a plain liver, and never wasted, or allowed others to waste any of his time, and these were direct aids to his success as a money maker. Some of the characteristics he possessed are worthy of imitation, and much needed in this country, to correct our expensive and extravagant habits.

The world was startled on December 4, 1891 when a homicidal maniac exploded a dynamite bomb in Mr Sage's office, following *One of Wall Street's* a demand for $1,200,000. Mr Sage suf-*most interesting figures.* fered little from the explosion, save the shock and some slight impairment to his hearing, but it is believed that the shock hastened the end of the life of one of Wall Street's most interesting figures and in his ninetieth year, Mr Sage passed away at his home on Long Island.

What was the secret of Sage's success? Certainly it differs radically from the characteristics of other big stock market operators. Mr Sage, when asked this question, referred his inquirer to the advice of Polonious to Laertes. Probably there is as much for those who would be successful in stock market operations to be gained from reading *Hamlet* as there is in the financial columns of the daily newspapers.

Nevertheless, the career of Mr Sage holds much for the public, as did Gould's. Sage was a professional bargain hunter. He knew values, and possessed that discernment of the relationship of market prices to intrinsic worth. He must have had infinite faith in America, one of the cardinal principles that makes for success in stock market operations. Sage knew that often, when a company was "down," it was far from "out." He must also have had vision, to foresee the needs of the country in transportation, in telegraph lines. This was a complement to his thrift. He saved his money, and when the time came to use it, he could pick and choose among the bargains in the securities market. It is said that in the most distressing times in the securities market, when prices were tumbling head over heels downward, "Uncle Russell" was always to be found among the heavy purchasers.

WILLIAM B. THOMPSON

*The history of the rise of the porphyry coppers, and
their great success in the securities market is in great
measure attributable to William B. Thompson.
As a market operator, as a mine maker, as a genius of
the Street, he stands aligned with the constructive
element. His doctrine of publicity has aided many
investors to success.*

WILLIAM B. THOMPSON

Stock market operators may be roughly divided into three classes: those who trade "all over the board," those who operate in a group of issues or a division of the market, and those who are irrevocably identified with a single issue, often for a lifetime. Of the first group, perhaps Livermore and Keene are the best examples; of the last Vanderbilt and Havemeyer are excellent types. It is more often, however, that we find market operators confining themselves to a single division of the market, such

Colonel Thompson may be credited with being one of the largest operators in mining securities.

as Gates with steel, Sage with railroads, or Colonel William Boyce Thompson with mining.

For Colonel Thompson may be credited with being one of the largest operators in mining securities during the past score of years. His name is coupled with some of the most conspicuous market successes, both in copper and silver stocks, especially the former, and during the period when America has risen to the position of supremacy in the copper world, through the development of the porphyry mines.

There are two outstanding characteristics of Colonel Thompson that have made for his success. One is thoroughness and the other is decision. He goes after the facts. He will spend thousands of dollars to get a single bit of information when he has decided that that information is the key to the proposition under investigation. He will never accept ready-made opinions. His method has been to dig and dig until he had every tiny fact in his possession and then come to an almost instantaneous decision – and he has rarely made mistakes.

He had been told that Inspiration was too low grade to make a copper mine. Inspiration today speaks for itself.

Of the other characteristic one has only to talk to him for a few minutes to realize the part that it plays in his character. His "yes" is a vigorous affirmative and his "no" is an equally emphatic negative. He may say either of them in a mild tone of voice with a smile in his blue eyes, but, having said it, you instantly realize that he is committed and he can't be budged.

Colonel Thompson, it is said, hates nothing so much as the "double cross." He is a builder and his wrath falls heavy on the man who would pull down the bricks when Thompson is engaged in putting up a financial structure. A story is told in the Street regarding a big market operation in a mining security, in the property of which some important developments had taken place and in which Thompson fully believed. The issue was selling at a modest price on the New York Curb Market and a large block of stock was owned by an official of the company. The stock had fallen into more or less disrepute, chiefly because of the fact that the public refused to believe in the future of the camp, owing to some adverse engineering reports, which were entirely premature and which are now the subject of ridicule among mining men, especially since the mines of the camp have yielded millions of dollars in dividends to the shareholders of the various companies.

Thompson believed the property was valuable. He approached the official with a view to buying his stock, but the official refused to name a price, stating, however, that he would not sell his securities if Thompson wanted to operate in the market and secure for himself the bulk of the floating supply at a reasonable figure. Thompson began buying at steadily rising prices and a genuine public interest was being created, when Thompson found that the official of the company was selling his stock to him.

Thompson sold every share that he owned, regardless of market price.

By the time the stock had risen to four times the figure at which Thompson had started buying it he found himself buying the official's stock in the open market and, the moment the first share came in, it is said that Thompson sold every share that he owned, regardless of market price. And Thompson never interested himself in that stock or that camp again. One must keep one's agreements, especially verbal ones, with William Boyce Thompson.

Colonel Thompson looks little of the part of the successful stock market operator. One sees as one enters his handsomely appointed and cheerful office, neither the grim-jawed, cold-blooded, stony-eyed hero of the fiction of ten years ago, nor the dark, nervous, slim, active type of the "movies." A little careless as to dress, for he likes comfort, with a round, smiling – one might almost say cherubic – countenance, radiating good nature, a low voice with a western drawl, a friendly, beaming smile – one might almost imagine he were a successful country doctor, instead of a financial power. One of his outstanding characteristics is his high courage. Thompson is the kind of a man who would approach a gang that tried to hold him up and, waving aside the pistols, sit down and talk things over. He had to do the same sort of thing with hostile banking interests. He is good natured and easy going and with a disarming amiability, but if it must be fight – Thompson can fight with two heavy hitting hands!

Colonel Thompson was born in Virginia City in 1869, three days after the driving of the gold spike that signaled the completion of the first transcontinental railroad. It may be literally said that mining was in his blood and his childhood was surrounded by all the picturesqueness of the frontier days, although the first boom of the Comstock had by that time petered out. It was a life of Daniel Webster he had read in his early years that fostered the idea of attending Exeter Academy and he came East in 1886. He had decided to make mining his career and began saturating himself, not only with the technical side of the industry through the study of metallurgy, but with practical field knowledge.

His father had moved to Butte and was developing a small number of claims and when Thompson left college, he went into the practical end of mining with his sire. He sold lumber, leased and worked claims, and mingled with the mining men. Even in those days his positive nature was asserting itself and the tremendous energy with which he assailed any project earned him the title of "Boulder" Thompson.

Colonel Thompson broke into the financial end of the mining business as many others have attempted and failed – only Thompson was successful. He came East representing a group of small mines seeking capital in the Street. Although a young man, he had found out that the East is likely to take one at one's own valuation. He did not whimperingly beg the world to take notice. He knocked with a thunderous knock and demanded that attention be paid to William Boyce Thompson and the financial world paid attention to William Boyce Thompson, because he was worth paying attention to.

He had courage on the top of an amazing groundwork of facts and it was not long before the name of Thompson was a synonym for success in the world of mining securities.

One of Colonel Thompson's first big successes was in Nevada Consolidated. He shared the vision of Daniel C. Jackling, the copper wizard, and believed with him that the big low grade *His operations in the* deposits of copper were to be the back-*market have never been* bone of the American copper industry. *of a secretive kind.* As Jackling worked with Utah Copper, so did Thompson work with Nevada Consolidated and, developing the property from a worthless, barren acreage into one of the big producing mines of America, he sold it to the Guggenheims at a huge profit.

Colonel Thompson has been identified with the stocks of many of the biggest mining enterprises in the country. His operations in the market have never been of a secretive kind. He is too much of a constructive force not to recognize the value of securing public cooperation, and when Thompson believed that market values were out of line with real values or prospective values, he usually told investors about it vigorously and persistently. Firms with

He knows that to attract capital is the true function of the stock market.

which Colonel Thompson has been identified, both in Boston and New York, have been credited with furnishing to the public the most accurate, concise, and easily assimilated information regarding mining properties that has ever been known in the Street and one suspects that it was Colonel Thompson's unusual clear-headedness and keen sense of the value of concerted public buying that directed the publicity of those organizations.

Colonel Thompson is more than a stock market operator. He knows that true standards of investment worth are established in the securities market. And he knows that to attract capital is the true function of the stock market. And, judging by his successes of the past, he wants to attract capital for those enterprises he relies on. He believes in keeping the public informed, down to the last detail, as to what the properties and their managements are doing. He knows that with an established market, and an open policy of publicity, investors will have confidence in the enterprise.

He keeps informed himself. He digests all the news, especially those items having a bearing on the enterprises in which he is interested. And those who remember his association with prominent stock brokerage houses prior to World War I, and during the period when the big porphyry mines were developing, have good cause to remember that the crisp analysis of corporate information and its probable effect on the value of securities was one of the most reliable and comprehensive pieces of financial publicity ever undertaken and carried out.

It is in this phase of his business ability that the world has come to know Thompson. Nevada Consolidated, Inspiration, Magma Copper, and others were given to the world through his genius. It has always been known that when Thompson is interested in the development of a property and invites the public to participate in its success, there is every reason to believe that it will be all the success he expects. His engineers have made examinations, and their reports must be voluminous as to detail, and accurate down to the last fraction. They must represent the most thorough investigation, and be the results of digging down to the bottom of things.

Prior to the war Colonel Thompson was a big outstanding figure in the Street. When the country called for men he promptly shut down his desk and plunged into the war's work. Prior to that time he had been engaged in the Belgian relief work. He was later given a commission with the American Red Cross Mission in Russia, of which he subsequently became the head.

After months of foreign service he came back, and with him he brought an idea that helped maintain the morale of the American Army in World War I, Thompson said:

"People away from home miss the home newspaper more than anything else."

The idea became a reality. It was a cure for a bad trouble – homesickness. He financed and organized a plan for sending the home paper to eight thousand of the boys at the front, and later had the idea adopted by four thousand newspapers all over the country.

He is a Republican. He was chairman of the Ways and Means Committee of the Republican National Committee in the campaign of 1920. He is stated to have played an important part in the creation and installation of the present Republican organization.

He has ever been an admirer of Theodore Roosevelt. Shortly after the war he became president of the Roosevelt Memorial Association, and is aiding materially in perpetuating the memory of the Great American.

The success of Colonel Thompson quickly attracted the attention of the leaders of the Street. His thoroughness of investigation, his ability to get "the truth, the whole truth and nothing but the truth" before he embarked in an enterprise, and his dogged persistence in carrying through what he believed in to the pinnacle of success drew the attention of the powers of Wall Street. So that in a short time Colonel Thompson found that he had associates even more powerful than he was. To him have been entrusted some of the most interesting market campaigns in mining securities. In the making of Inspiration, Thompson was aligned with the greatest banking interests in the country.

Some years ago Colonel Thompson was mentioned early and often on the financial pages of the public press in connection with the enterprises with which he was associated and shouldering upward to success. Of recent years, however, he is staying somewhat in the background, hiding from the limelight of publicity, although he is understood to be even more active in the markets than ever. He still retains an interest in those companies which he has made, but is ever seeking new fields.

It is said that he is materially interested in the developments of the sulphur deposits of Texas. He is rumored to be occupied with the development of the Canadian gold fields. His engineers are said to be conducting a series of investigations of mining properties in China which may lead to the development of an astonishing silver property. He is also reported to be heavily interested in the South African gold properties.

He has become somewhat more elusive, but the old characteristics prevail. His investigations are more thorough, and once he is satisfied he will probably go ahead, and, as usual, the investing public will have an opportunity to sit in with him in his ventures and successes.

Many of Colonel Thompson's great successes started on the New York Curb Market. After two or three had fulfilled their promise, marketwise, he built up a great following, both among the traders and the investing public. The confirmation of the report that W. B. Thompson was interested in the prospect was almost certain to give it a hall-mark. And the Street whispers that he is still, and will probably always be more or less identified with the activity in good mining securities in the junior market.

STEPHEN V. WHITE

"Deacon" White was one of the most courageous of
Wall Street's knights. To have lost everything at the age
of sixty would have broken the spirit of a man of less
heroic stature.
But White, with the spirit of one of his ancestors,
Cromwell, behind him, turned his defeat into a
glorious victory – an achievement that has a high place
in the Street's annals.

STEPHEN V. WHITE

....

Big men of Wall Street have no common proving ground that fits them for the market. Few of the big operators have been men of erudition. Many of the old-timers had only the crudest and roughest of schooling. Thus, Daniel Drew was a drover, Thompson was a miner, Flower a politician. Livermore, it is true, was almost suckled on ticker tape. But the Street draws from all the professions and industries, from the soil and the city, from the country schoolhouse and the college.

But as one traces back the ancestry of many of the Wall Street geniuses, one finds a majority of them have sprung from farming people. Something seems to give those whose forebears were of *The most dramatic spot is Wall Street, and a chief actor in the drama is Stephen V. White.* the soil a surer grasp on the secrets of money-making and financial construction, than those whose parents are of the cities, where small things obscure the broader vision and where ideals fade quickly. And like many of those who reached a dominant position in Wall Street affairs, Stephen V. (Deacon) White came from the wilderness.

Twenty years ago, Frank A. Munsey said:

> There is always something interesting about genius, in whatever capacity it shows itself. The time was when the soldier, the poet, the orator, the jurist, the sculptor, the painter, were almost alone endowed with genius. That was before the days of the financier. In

this country of ours, where the spirit of money getting is the most marked national characteristic, where dollars, with the average degree of refinement and good sense, bring social position and luxuries and comforts – including such ornamental properties as titled sons-in-law – here it is that genius asserts itself in the financier and becomes most forceful and most dramatic. The most dramatic spot on this earth today is Wall Street, and a chief actor in the drama that is enacted there daily is Stephen V. White.

Stephen V. White at that time had shown himself to be one of the strongest, squarest, and most able stock market operators in the Street. A few months before he had created a tremendous bull market in grain, which market had collapsed under terrific pressure from Chicago and New York operators, and the breaking of which had carried away White's entire fortune, bankrupted him, and left him $1,000,000 in debt.

He was forced to discontinue his operations in the market, but White had built up a tremendous following and, a few months later, so great was the belief on the part of his creditors in Stephen White's genius that they came to him and said:

"Mr White, your assets would pay us about 55% in cash of our entire claims against your firm, but it is our pleasure to give you back your business and to cancel your obligations to us, leaving you free from indebtedness and with a handsome capital with which to resume business."

It was a magnificent tribute and White's answer reveals the qualities of the man in what may be considered one of the most beautiful utterances in the annals of the Street. Mr White said:

A word of recognition of the unparalleled forbearance and kindness of the creditors of S. V. White & Co. is due you, and as the embarrassment to my firm was my personal act, a personal statement from me seems to be most appropriate. The legal release of all indebtedness, which you have given, imposes a four-fold debt in that jurisprudence where honor issues her decrees. I wish to say that the estate about to be returned shall be accepted as a trust to be administered under that sacred code which honor imposes, and, if life is spared, I have no fear of your ultimate loss. And so with thanks beyond expression, with humility too profound to be removed even by the peerless and priceless compliment of your continued confidence, I take up my work anew, with the determination to so conduct it that, when the summons shall come to pay the debt of nature, it shall be the only debt remaining unpaid.

Moreover, he meant every word of it. He was readmitted to trading, taking his stand at the old Delaware, Lackawanna & Western post, with which security he was identified during practically all of his active life in the Street. In two days he made a profit of over $12,000 and before the second day was over, he had paid every creditor whose claim was under $500. In eleven months, he had cleared the slate. Not a penny was lost by those who believed in "Deacon" White's integrity.

Stephen Van Culen White was born in Chatham County, North Carolina, on August 1, 1831. His mother, Julia Brewer, was a direct descendant of Oliver Cromwell and a member of the old North Carolina family of that name. His father, Hiram White, was a North Carolina farmer, but shortly after young Stephen was born, the family being hostile to slavery, moved to Jersey County,

Illinois and Stephen spent his boyhood in what was then a wilderness.

The commercial instinct in young White was developed at an early age, when he made money from the sale of furs, the product of his own traps. The Illinois River bottom lands were then alive with small animals and in Stephen's trapping and in the sales of skins to the American Fur Co. dawned his business instincts. In 1884 he entered the preparatory school of Knox College at Galesburg, Illinois and worked his way through by teaching school to pay his expenses, graduating in 1854. From there he went to St Louis as a bookkeeper in the office of Claflin, Allen & Stinde, a mercantile firm, when law attracted him and he studied with Brown and Kasson, the latter member of the firm being John D. Kasson, who was afterwards United States Minister to Germany. Incidentally he dipped into the newspaper profession, writing editorials and reviews for the *Missouri Democrat*, the proceeds of which helped pay his way, while he was getting ready for admission to the bar, to which he was admitted in 1856.

White then went to Des Moines, Iowa and engaged in successful practice and in 1864 he served for a time as United States District Attorney for Iowa, during the illness of the incumbent of the office.

It was in 1865 that Mr White came to New York, where, although continuing his practice of law, his commercial and financial strength found an opportunity to broaden. And one finds him shortly afterward establishing, with Charles B. Marvin, the stock brokerage and banking firm of Marvin & White. Although from this point in Mr White's history, he was identified almost exclusively with Wall Street activities, he frequently appeared as counsel in the federal courts and sometimes in the Supreme Court of the United States.

After a few years, subsequent to the formation of the firm of Marvin & White, Mr Marvin withdrew and Mr White continued

The "Deacon" was always to be found on the constructive side of the market.

alone until 1881, when he established the firm of S. V. White & Co. with several partners. The firm was always more or less identified with the activities in Delaware, Lackawanna & Western, a property and security that Mr White always believed in, and the "Deacon" was always to be found on the constructive site of the market. In fact, the greater part of Mr White's successful operations were on the long side of the market, which identifies him with the builders of America's financial and industrial structure.

A story was recently told by a veteran of Wall Street regarding a market operation of White's, that reveals something of the manner in which stock market operators work. It must be remembered that White was a contemporary of a group of powerful financiers operating in "pet" issues. To be on the right side of a movement in a stock meant an opportunity for handsome profits. The "tip" was more the currency of the Street than it is today. One day a young friend of White's rushed into his office, bursting with the information that one of the men controlling a big industrial, together with his market associates, was buying the stock for one of its characteristic rises, which usually meant somewhere between

30 and 50 points. The young man apparently had correct information (he was in a state of extreme excitement) and urged White to buy – and buy heavily.

Imagine his dismay when, after listening calmly to his story, White called his chief clerk and ordered him to sell a big block of the stock. Immediately White stepped to the ticker and literally watched the stock sold. When the sale was reported to him, he ordered another similar block sold. By this time the young man was nearly paralyzed. After the two large blocks had been sold and White had carefully scrutinized the transactions as they appeared on the tape, the "Deacon" immediately gave orders to buy many times the number of shares he had sold.

The true test was in the market itself.

White took the trouble to explain.

He said that, while the information might have been correct, the true test was in the market itself. The first block of stock had been absorbed easily. The second was taken at advancing prices. It was then plainly written on the tape that the crowd operating in the security were buying for a big rise and were willing to take all stock offered. And White decided to go with the tide.

Just how much White made out of the transaction is not told, but his explanation furnishes a sidelight on just how and why a big market operator takes a position in the market.

Although White was a keen, practical financier and lawyer, he was nevertheless quite a scholar. He was well versed in the classics and was especially fond of astronomy, having a fine observatory in his home in Brooklyn. At one time he was Park Commissioner of

Brooklyn and in 1886 was elected to Congress from his home city.

It was in Brooklyn that he acquired the title of "Deacon." There were two reasons why he came to be known by this familiar name. One was his appearance, the quiet, elderly, scholarly type. But the real basis was his active membership in the Plymouth Congregational Church of Brooklyn, although he never held the position of deacon of the church. He was, however, a warm, personal friend of Henry Ward Beecher, who is described by one of his biographers as "that grand old Chrysostom of the nineteenth century, who left the world brighter for his memory and darker for his absence." The scholarly White and the ardent cleric had many qualities in common that made them close friends.

Deacon White was a bold and fearless operator. He had that element of courage that is necessary to the successful consummation of big transactions. His judgment was unusually sound and he *It symbolizes the great* would often back up his opinions with *essential of successful* the weight of his entire fortune. It is *market operations –* said that, even in the operation in grain, *Courage.* which temporarily downed him, he could have successfully combatted the frontal attack of the big professional bear operators, had it not been combined with the treachery of one of his employees, who aided his enemies and weakened his position.

At that time White was 60 years old. He was a veteran of many Wall Street battles and of one previous financial disaster, in which his capital was wiped out, but in which incident every debt was paid. It must be a magnificent character that can, at the age of three score, see every dollar of a big fortune disappear and face a million dollars' worth of debts, only to take up the broken tools, wipe out the indebtedness and build another fortune. It symbolizes the great essential of successful market operations – Courage.

CHARLES F. WOERISHOFFER

*Persistence forms the basis of the success of
Woerishoffer. Single handed he achieved victories over
the most sagacious operators in the market that
brought him not only fame but a fortune.
Unlike others who have swayed the market,
Woerishoffer drove it, browbeat it, and whipped it, his
operations being of an astonishing magnitude. His
short stormy career forms an unusually interesting
page of Wall Street history.*

CHARLES F. WOERISHOFFER

M any and diverse are the characteristics of the men who have swayed the stock market. One big operator will coax it; another will lift it bodily in a burst of enthusiasm; still another would undermine it; one will lead it up step by step, gathering strength all the way. But few have possessed the power to lash it, browbeat it, bully it, as did Charles F. Woerishoffer.

The market operations of the "Baron," as he was familiarly called, were born out of that peculiar combination of German phlegm and American nervousness, aided by great perspicacity, *If the market failed to* that produced extraordinary results. *obey, Woerishoffer used* Woerishoffer said to the market, *the whip.* "jump," and if the market failed to obey, Woerishoffer used the whip. He was devoid of fear. He backed that almost irresistible combination of Jay Gould and Russell Sage into a corner and made them eat out of his hand. It was a feat that brought him tremendous prestige.

It has been said that Woerishoffer was a great bear. An analysis of his operations does not confirm the accusation. He was on both sides of the market as the opportunity presented. For Woerishoffer, if anything, was an opportunist. He crossed swords with the biggest operators of his time, including Gould, Sage, Villard, Keene, White, and Morgan.

A contemporary said of him at the time of his death in 1886:

The results of his life work show what can be accomplished by any man who sets himself at work upon an idea, and who devotes himself steadily and persistently to a course of action for the development and perfection of the principle which actuates his life. Mr Woerishoffer possessed peculiar personal qualities, which are denied to most men and to all women. He had the magnetic power of impressing people with confidence in the schemes which he inaugurated; that is to say, he had the power of organization – the same power has made other men great, and will continue to make men great who possess it in all walks of life.

Charles F. Woerishoffer was born at Glenhauser in the Province of Hess, Germany, in 1844. His family were poor but very worthy and reputable people and had no means to give Charles a start in business life. The struggle for existence at an early age forced him to depend upon himself from early boyhood and served to develop his self-reliance, his enterprise, and his habit of independent thinking – three characteristics which dominated his later successful business career. His early training was in Frankfurt and Paris and in 1865 he sailed for America, to seek his fortune. He settled in New York City in the office of August Rutten, as a clerk. His ability was not to be hidden long and he was soon made cashier.

The ambitious young man at the age of 24, started out for himself with M. C. Klingenfeldt and about a year later, became a member of the stock exchange. His first big business was for L. Von Hoffman & Co. They found young Woerishoffer trustworthy, energetic, and prudent and gradually threw an increasing volume of business his way. The financial results of this success were the foundation of his fortune.

In the summer of 1870, he organized the firm of Woerishoffer & Co. as stockbrokers and bankers, his first partners being Messrs Schromberg and Schuyler. The new firm was successful from the start and Schromberg and Schuyler soon retired with substantial fortunes.

Woerishoffer in five years had developed from a poor immigrant into a rising young banker and broker.

Woerishoffer, besides being a bold operator, was associated with the large railroad construction in the United States. He was connected with the Northern Pacific, Ontario & Western, West Shore, Oregon Transcontinental, Mexican National, and Denver & Rio Grande. He was, as a matter of fact, one of the

When the market began its great upward movement, Woerishoffer was a member of one of the big bull cliques.

first to propose the building of the Denver & Rio Grande, and in its making, Woerishoffer realized very substantial profits for himself and his associates.

In 1878, when the market began its great upward movement on account of the general prosperity of the country, Woerishoffer was a member of one of the big bull cliques. It was at this time that the "Baron" became a millionaire. It took 13 years from the time of his entrance to America to accumulate his first million, but a million dollars in those days was a lot of money and the possessors of that sum were few and far between.

It was in 1879 that Woerishoffer showed his mettle. He had

developed the confidence of foreign investors to a degree that he became the representative of the Frankfurt investors in Kansas Pacific. Woerishoffer had contracted to sell a large number of bonds to a syndicate headed by Gould and Sage at 80. The Gould-Sage interests had decided to welch on their contract with Woerishoffer and stated that they came to the conclusion, after examining the roadbed, that the bonds were not worth more than 70 and would not take them at a higher figure.

Woerishoffer retired from his defeat gracefully, but immediately cabled the English and German bondholders and very shortly had a majority of the bonds which the syndicate wanted in his possession. These were deposited with the United States Trust Co. He then notified the syndicate that they could not obtain a single bond under par to carry out their scheme. Gould and Sage winced but capitulated, and in Woerishoffer's triumph, he is said to have not only netted over $1,000,000, but to have gained a tremendous following in Germany and England.

Thus Woerishoffer jumped into international prominence as a far sighted operator, and was responsible for a flow of English and German capital into the American market and into American enterprises.

It is related that the combination of Gould and Sage was brought about as a defence against Woerishoffer and Keene. Keene had come to New York and made mistakes that had cost him a great deal of money, but he was sharpening his teeth and, together with Woerishoffer, made an attack on Gould that caused him to dodge behind Sage's millions.

Woerishoffer with his persistence and energy and Keene with his cunning represented a combination that even the astute and clever Gould could not withstand alone.

The worsting of Henry Villard by Woerishoffer forms one of the triumphs of the latter's career. Villard had formed a blind pool, with Woerishoffer and others, for the purpose of gaining control of Northern Pacific, in order that it might be consolidated with Oregon Railway & Navigation Co. and other interests and build up an immense transportation system.

Woerishoffer, according to the story told at the time, did not countenance the artificial forcing of the price of Northern Pacific upward. Villard accused him of selling the stock short and demanded that he withdraw from the pool. Woerishoffer promptly agreed and Villard, believing him to be short of a great block of Northern Pacific, formed a syndicate for the purpose of acquiring 100,000 shares of stock and squeezing Woerishoffer out of the market.

The worsting of Henry Villard by Woerishoffer forms one of the triumphs of the latter's career.

There were various millionaires and prominent financiers in the syndicate and Woerishoffer had thrown down the gage of battle to a group of the most prominent operators in the Street. The buying of Northern Pacific began and by the time 20,000 shares were bought, funds in the hands of the syndicate began to get low. More money, more influence, and more power were drawn to the syndicate and a determined effort was made to squeeze Woerishoffer on what they believed to be a big line of stocks. When the battle was over, it was found that the last 80,000 shares of stock had been bought from Woerishoffer and that, instead of being short of the stock, he had been long and had sold Villard and his crowd the stock, while Woerishoffer got the money.

Woerishoffer netted millions of dollars in this transaction in 1883 and it is considered one of the best planned and most dramatic victories ever accomplished single handed in the annals of Wall Street.

Personally Woerishoffer was not to be picked out from the crowd as a man of financial boldness. He was slightly built and of a characteristic light, Teutonic complexion, bespectacled and with a mustache such as many men of the period affected, and one might have taken him for an inconsequential bank clerk. He was, however, a born gambler and one might find him after the battle *Charles Woerishoffer's* in the Street was done, at Long Branch, *operations in the Street* then very much "wide open" and the *were of an unusual* center of the sporting fraternity of the *magnitude for the* country, playing faro. And when *period.* Woerishoffer played it was for big stakes, and he is reported to have broken the bank twice at one of the then famous gambling institutions of New Jersey. He was also a good poker player and would often take a turn at roulette.

Woerishoffer, like Keene, was extremely charitable. It is said that he made presents to faithful brokers of over twenty seats on the exchange, then having a value of $25,000 each. He made a present of a $500 horse to the cabman who drove him daily to and from his office. His generosity to his employees made them the most envied of all that great army that toil in Wall Street.

Usually he possessed a Teutonic phlegm that exhibited itself most plainly when the battle was waging fiercest. It is said that, during the memorable campaign with Villard, his coolness and composure were in striking contrast to the vigor of the battle he was waging. Occasionally signs of the mental strain would creep out in a spasm of nervousness, but these occasions were rare.

In 1875, he married Miss Annie Uhl, the stepdaughter of Oswald Ottendorfer, editor and proprietor of the great New York German newspaper, the *Staats-Zeitung*. It is understood that Miss Uhl brought him a fortune of $300,000.

Charles Woerishoffer's operations in the Street were of an unusual magnitude for the period. It was thought at the time that in his efforts to dominate the situation and drive the market his

He was alternately on the bear side and the bull side. way, the volume of his transactions grew out of a careless mind. A contemporary, writing some years after his death, stated that he did not believe Mr Woerishoffer ever undertook a speculation of any sort until he had carefully calculated all the chances. "His success, remarkable as it was, was due to the combination of calculation and the natural development of business conditions, of which he was a close student."

One of Mr Woerishoffer's remarkable attributes was his skill in putting other operators off the track of his operations, by employing a large number of brokers and by changing his brokers and the seat of his operations so often that those who attempted to follow him were unable to discern his next move or discover what he was going to do. He was alternately on the bear side and the bull side. And very often when he was reputed to be a tremendous seller of securities, he was accumulating large blocks of stock.

Charles F. Woerishoffer made one mistake and, had it not been for his sudden end, he would have probably lost his entire fortune. He was heavily committed to the short side of the market during a period of the country's progress and expansion. It may be pointed out, however, that just prior to his end, he felt that he had overexercised his faculties and his constitution was beginning to break down under the strain. He decided to visit Europe for the purpose of recuperating and it was probably in this strained mental condition that he failed to get the clear view of the country's progress.

It was the beginning of a bull cycle, but Woerishoffer, with his characteristic persistence, attempted to go against the tide. He might drive the market, but he could not drive the United States, with its tremendous resources, its huge productive capacity, its astounding recuperative power – for those were the influences that were then at work on securities values and which no market operator may turn back, any more than King Canute could turn back the sea.

ADDISON CAMMACK

*One of the ablest of the "freelance" operators of his
time, Addison Cammack was one of the first men to
realize the importance of market "cycles."
With little or nothing to start on, Cammack, in his
twenty-two years of market operations, made
$10,000,000. He was essentially an opportunist, and
coupled with a broad vision, keen perception, and
courage, pulled himself up the ladder of success.*

ADDISON CAMMACK

....

Ⅰn reviewing the history of successful operators in Wall Street it is apparent at once that the "freelance" has the hardest task.

Successful operations that must be born out of an ability to read the tape, to judge values from the action of the market, from the *It has been said that* course of the country's progress, from *"the tape never lies".* an intimate knowledge of world affairs, from a thousand-and-one signs – require not only an unusual mentality, but diligent application to the subject.

It has been said that "the tape never lies." All of which may be true, but the tape has a way of speaking in language that may not be understood by the reader. And often the tape talks ambiguously, as any stock market operator will tell you.

The big operator who is allied with certain interests, and has at his command information that is not for general publication, has a simple task compared with the "freelance," the outsider, who must get his inspiration sometimes from the signs and figures on the board, or, what has been more often the case, from within, in the guise of "hunches," intuition, or other forms of inspiration.

Before Livermore, who is the highest living type of market student, there was Keene, but contemporary with Keene there was that famous quartet of operators – one of the most powerful of their time – Woerishoffer, Smith, Osborne, and Addison Cammack.

And of these four, Cammack is the outstanding figure. He played a lone hand most of the time – and he played it with

Either side of the market appealed to him.

courage and daring, with nerve and with secrecy. When Cammack withdrew from the market, it was his boast that he had made a fortune of $10,000,000 in his twenty-two years of market activity.

Like others who play a lone hand, Cammack was an opportunist. Either side of the market appealed to him, as the opportunity presented itself. He was on the constructive side of the market in some of the greatest movements in the Street. On the other hand, he was aligned with Woerishoffer in the pricking of the Villard bubble. For sheer nerve he was unequalled, even by that master of courage, Jay Gould, who, it is said, intensely admired Cammack and the daring of his operations. But if Cammack was courageous, it was the courage born of the conviction that he was right. Like Davy Crockett, he first made sure that he was right, and then went ahead, with all the power at his command.

In the time of Cammack and his contemporaries, groups of

Cammack actually created a tremendous buying power in the market.

securities moved together. Thus, if one mid-western railroad showed unusual strength, there was bound to be a reflection of this strength in other roads in the same group. Cammack took advantage of this fact.

Thus, he would quietly accumulate a long line of various railroad stocks all in a single group, buying quietly and persistently, and using many brokers to cover his operations. When his line of stocks was complete, he would select a road that he had not yet touched, and buy heavily and openly. Cammack had a substantial following, who figured that if Cammack were buying one of the group, he must have inside information that would probably cause an advance in the whole collection.

The result was that Cammack actually created a tremendous buying power in the market, and when the price rose, he would quietly sell the securities he had accumulated, netting huge profits thereon. The stock he had bought openly, and which had been made the leader of the movement, he would dispose of for what he could. It mattered not whether he sustained a loss in that issue; his profits were in the advance in the other securities in the group.

Addison Cammack was born in Hopkinsville, Kentucky. His father was a farmer and his early life was amid humble circumstances. He began his business career as a clerk in the office of J. P. Whitney & Co., ship brokers of New Orleans. In 1861 the name

Addison Cammack participated in some of the biggest market movements of his time.

of the firm was changed to Cammack & Converse, successors to J. P. Whitney & Co. Mr Cammack was an intimate friend of Nelson C. Trowbridge and of Charles Lamar, who was a relative of L. Q. C. Lamar, Secretary of the Interior in President Cleveland's administration.

Cammack's enemies in the Street used to circulate a venomous story (especially at times when Cammack had worsted them in the market) that he was interested in the slave trade. Trowbridge and Lamar owned a yacht called *The Wanderer* and in 1859 it brought 600 negroes to Savannah. Cammack's friendship for the two men undoubtedly led to the linking of his name with the story, but those who knew Mr Cammack before he came north thoroughly denounced the insinuation as a slander, utterly devoid of foundation. During the early part of the war, Mr Cammack lived in Savannah and in 1863 he went to England and remained a year. In 1866 he came to New York and engaged in the liquor business with J. W. George. A few years later, Mr Cammack entered Wall Street, forming a partnership with Charles J. Osborne under the name of Osborne & Cammack. This partnership was very successful and was, after a few years, dissolved, when Mr Cammack became an independent market operator.

Addison Cammack during his activity in the Street, participated in some of the biggest market movements of his time. It is said that his first big fortune was made in connection with the consolidation of the West Shore and the New York Central, which terminated a long and bitter railroad war and which sent the prices of all railroad stocks up vigorously. He was at this time aligned with the Vanderbilt interests and it was one of the very few times in his career when he was associated with the "inside interests of any

He was one of the earliest to recognize the importance of business cycles in affecting the market.

big corporation." Cammack, it is said, was quick to perceive what peace in the railroad world would mean to railroad stocks in general and bought to the limit of his resources.

A contemporary in recounting a story of Cammack's able operations in railroad securities says: "From all I have heard, I am inclined to think that Cammack was one of the ablest stock traders the Street ever saw. He was not a chronic bear. . . . He is credited with coining the warning, 'Don't sell stocks when the sap is running up the trees' and the old timers tell me that his biggest winnings were made on the bull side, so that it is plain he did not play prejudices, but conditions. At all events he was a consummate trader."

Cammack was a student of other things beside the tape. He was one of the earliest to recognize the importance of business cycles in affecting the market and his great standby was a book known as *Benner's Prophecies*. Benner was an Ohio farmer, who made a study of prices and Cammack is said to be the first man to figure out the long swing movements in stock prices – to study market cycles and to gauge the effect of the tide of business upon security values.

He was a big trader in his day. His operations reached a magnitude of unusual proportions for a "freelance." While such men as Vanderbilt, Gould, and others directly interested in railroad properties might trade in thousands of shares of their pet security, it was rare that an independent operator would step into the market as sometimes Cammack did, and buy 50,000 shares in a single day. It must be remembered that the number of shares listed on the market in those days was much smaller than it is today.

Cammack was tall, well built, and was probably one of the gruffest personalities in the Street. Behind that gruffness, however, which was more or less assumed and which served as a rebuff to those who were trying to worm out of him his moves in the market, there existed a chivalry and courtesy that came of a good heart. He was strong-willed, as shown by the fact that all his life he was an inveterate smoker and when his doctor told him that smoking was harmful, he stopped short. He was a dyed-in-the-wool Democrat and was a heavy contributor to the Cleveland campaign in 1884. He was to be seen very often in the Windsor Hotel in New York. It was then "uptown" and was the center of a great deal of stock market activity as well as the meeting place for many large market operators.

He was always the center of a listening group, each trying to guess what he meant by what he did not say. Cammack was so successful that his every move was watched, but be it to his credit that he kept the Street guessing most of the time, for he recognized that one tiny indication might lead to a host of would-be followers, "beating him to the punch."

One who was associated with him in his market operations said at the time Cammack was extremely active in the Street:

"In manners he is very democratic and candid, and occasionally somewhat bluff; but he is a man of generous impulses, very charitable, and has plenty of friends, both for his financial acumen and for his qualities as a man who never deserts his friends, and who has not a few of the characteristics of mediaeval chivalry joined to the shrewd practicality of a great stock operator of this practical epoch."

So mysterious were Cammack's operations, that at the time he sold his seat in February 1894, the Street believed it was a piece of speculative strategy and were looking for some sensational developments, such as Cammack had furnished the market during the twenty-two years he had been intimately associated with it. But Cammack was through. He had made during his Wall Street activity some $10,000,000. But at the time he left the Street, he was reputed to be worth $2,500,000. As a. matter of fact, Mr Cammack retired from the Street at the desire of his wife, who thought that he had reached a time of life when he should give up business altogether. He was then seventy-one years old and did not look a day over fifty, and his mentality and perspicacity were as keen as they were when he first entered the big arena.

He was married when he was sixty, his wife having been a Miss Hildreth of Washington. He had two children, both boys, and on his marriage, it is said, he presented his wife with securities worth $1,000,000, thereafter placing considerable real estate in her name. Every dollar of his wealth he accumulated himself.

The career of Cammack illustrates what can be done single-handed in the market. Cammack had little or nothing to start on. His first speculative operations were in cotton, having been attracted to the commodity by his southern birth. From operations in a commodity, it is but a step to securities.

Cammack saw in the collapse in market values the vision of better times.

Cammack saw opportunities. He was not only able to read the signs of the times, to judge the progress of the country, but was able to read in the course of the market, the operations of the leaders. And he was wise enough to align himself on the right side.

Probably this is best shown in the period that followed "Black Friday." Cammack saw in the prices established in that memorable collapse in market values, the vision of better times. He accurately judged the future of the country. He was quick to recognize that a new cycle was at hand, based upon the recuperative powers of the United States, and that, in that new era of business, there would be a reflection of the business prosperity in the market. Henry N. Smith, with whom he had been associated, did not share the vision. Cammack tried to show him, but Smith fought the rising tide, with the result that he was practically ruined.

Cammack had, in addition to his great ability to read and understand the market, that asset that all who would be success-ful market operators must have – a broad-gauge vision of the country as a whole, its almost illimitable natural wealth, its abil-ity to recover from the most staggering blows. Such vision leads to success.

F. AUGUSTUS HEINZE

*The tale of Fritz Augustus Heinze is one of near
success. It is a story of a big man with a weak spot in
his armor. Master of Butte Geology, perpetual litigant,
his career was one of the most dramatic in mining
financial history. His operations in copper stocks on
the New York Curb Market are still remembered for
their magnitude.*

F. AUGUSTUS HEINZE

....

It takes many elements to assure success in stock market operations. As one reads the stories of the operations of the masters of the market, one recognizes that courage, vision, study,

Woe to the operator who regards his success too long in his mirror. confidence in oneself, an ability to about-face in moments of crisis – all play their parts. One of the chief essentials, however, is mental balance. Woe to the operator who regards his success too long in his mirror. He must be ever watchful of his mental attitude. He must, above all things, never fool himself, though he may dupe his enemies in the market.

There have been many who have climbed close to the pinnacle of success only to fall because of overconfidence. One of the shrewdest operators the New York Curb Market has ever seen has gone down to defeat five different times, because he believed he was greater than the market. His ability to gauge markets is almost uncanny, his courage tremendous, yet some curious kink in his brain warps his judgment at a crucial time, and his belief in himself reaches absurd heights – resulting in inevitable disaster.

The really great man knows when to run. Those who have achieved success instantaneously realize when to swell themselves to Brobdingnagian proportions, and when to assume Lilliputian size.

In previous stories of stock market operators, there has always been present the element of success. But for each successful one, there are ten who go up like a rocket and down like the stick. Some element is missing. The stories of the near-great would fill a volume. For the purpose of illustration, therefore, of the other side of stock market operations, this shall be the story of one whose career was spectacular, whose market operations were successful to a certain point, who had all the elements of being a market master – but slipped. He was a contemporary of many of the old traders in the market of the present generation – Fritz Augustus Heinze.

Heinze was a strikingly handsome man. He had the gift of oratory and might have made a great success as a minister of the gospel, had he followed the calling marked out for him by his *Heinze's brilliant career* parents. Magnetic, with a keen mind, *was terminated by the* daring, ambitious, and possessing *spectacular crash in the* unbounded confidence in his own abil- *market in 1907.* ity, Heinze had no thought of limiting himself to the narrow confines of the Lutheran ministry. From a mining engineer to a mine owner, to a champion of mining litigation, to a multi-millionaire, to a powerful stock market operator at the age of 38, Heinze's brilliant career was terminated by the spectacular crash in the market in 1907, which wiped out practically his entire fortune, closing up banks and trust companies and precipitating a financial panic.

There is both tribute and bitterness in Thomas W. Lawson's description of this "young Lochinvar who came out of the West" and the following must be read with the knowledge that Lawson and Heinze were on opposite sides of the fence. He says:

He had ability akin to genius of the order that wins eminence in bunco and confidence operations; boundlessly ambitious, inordinately egotistical, he was utterly devoid of moral perception. Among the keepers of gambling hells and barrooms, he was reckoned a prince of good fellows. Even in those days before he had made his first strike for fortune, Heinze's colossal egotism, which is of the I-must-be-in-the-limelight-when-it-strikes-the-grand-stand order, had made itself felt. This overweening vanity is the keynote of Heinze's makeup. Popularity is the breath of his nostrils.

One gets the picture, between the lines, of a great figure, of strong personality, of intense magnetism, of high courage, which impression gains strength as one reads the history of Heinze's spectacular career, the life of a stormy petrel.

Heinze's father was an importer and the head of a prosperous concern in Brooklyn. The family lived in an aristocratic section of the city and Fritz Augustus was born on December 5, 1869. The elder Heinze, as each of his sons became old enough to go to school, sent them to Germany. First went Otto, then Arthur, and then Fritz Augustus when he was nine years old. They attended school at Hildesheim and when Fritz came back from school at the age of 15, he said to his mother, "I am going to call myself Augustus, not Fritz. Before I went to Germany, the boys here called me German Fritz and in Germany they call me Yankee Frank."

And ever afterward, he was known as F. Augustus Heinze. On his return from Germany, he was sent to Brooklyn Polytechnic Institute and then to Columbia University and took a mining engineering course. On graduation he went to Butte, Montana, where he got a job as inside engineer for the old Boston & Montana Co. (later to become a part of Amalgamated Copper) at $5 a day. He worked eleven hours a day and worked hard. But he always dressed well and was nicknamed "The Dude." For five years Heinze pegged away at his work and made himself a master of intimate knowledge of the ore systems of the famous Butte Hill. It is probable that no contemporary had as concise and accurate a knowledge of the great ore systems of Butte, as did F. Augustus Heinze. Then his grandmother died and left him $50,000 and he came East.

His brother, Arthur, was then practicing law and Fritz took Arthur back to Butte with him. The two formed a perfect complement. Fritz knew the ore and Arthur knew the law. Between the two they tied Butte up in a mess of litigation, from which it took years for the big camp to disentangle itself. Heinze's first victory was over James A. Murray, in the lease on the Estrella claim. With the profits from the Estrella, he bought control of the Rarus Mine. Then he got hold of the Glengarry Mine and built a big smelter. His next venture was in British Columbia where he built a smelter at Trail City and a narrow gauge railroad to Rossland. He got control of the Leroy Mine, and promised to become so formidable a power in the territory that the Canadian Pacific paid $1,200,000 for his property and was glad to get rid of him.

Then came the famous Butte litigation, in which Heinze crossed swords with the Standard Oil interests. This was in 1897 when he was only 28 years old, but was recognized as one of the ablest mining men in that section of the country. Heinze had pushed down from the Rarus mine into the Michael Davitt claim owned by Butte & Boston and on the other side into a property owned by the Boston & Montana. Both companies sued him and as both were owned by Marcus Daly, it was expected that Heinze would get thoroughly licked. Then followed the formation of *Everywhere* Amalgamated Copper when Daly died *Amalgamated turned,* and Heinze fought Amalgamated as *there was Heinze.* keenly as he fought Daly. In a short time he had sixty lawsuits all going simultaneously. His brother dug into the title of every claim owned by Amalgamated and whenever there was a flaw, there was a suit.

Everywhere Amalgamated turned, there was Heinze. In February 1906, the Amalgamated interests attempted to compromise, but Amalgamated was thinking in terms of hundreds of thousands of dollars, while Heinze was thinking in millions. Heinze took it to the courts and the net result was that Heinze came out victorious with some $12,000,000.

He was only 28 years old, a rosy faced boy. He was hail-fellow-well-met with everybody and made friends rapidly. He was called the handsomest man in the state and he looked the part, standing five feet, ten inches in height, weighing 200 pounds, with the torso of a Yale halfback, muscles of steel, a face of ivory whiteness, lighted up with a pair of large blue eyes. Heinze conquered the feminine portion of the rough mining camp without effort. The young engineer was a fine musician, a brilliant linguist and, when necessary, could box like a professional. The conflict in Butte showed that in spite of all his gaiety, no man ever went underground who had a more intimate knowledge of the orebodies of Butte.

Flushed with his victories, Heinze came east to conquer the financial world. What had been done with Amalgamated Copper, he would do with United Copper, into which all his properties were put and which was launched on the New York Curb as a rival to the big Standard Oil combination. He became identified with market movements in copper stocks. He established his

His millions were welcome in the Street, but Heinze was not.

brothers, Otto and Arthur, in the brokerage business under the name of Otto C. Heinze & Co. He essayed to become a financial leader. He acquired banks and was elected the director of several mining companies. His operations in copper stocks grew. He brought Ohio Copper and Davis Daly to the attention of the public. His operations in these, in United Copper, in Stewart Mining, and others attracted a tremendous following. It looked as though Heinze were to be Wall Street's leader in the coppers.

But Heinze's old enemies had not forgotten. His millions were welcome in the Street, but Heinze was not. Traps were laid for him. He was plotted against. And had it not been for his excessive confidence in himself, he would have seen the handwriting on the wall of the catastrophe of 1907.

Heinze believed in his properties and he believed in himself. He believed that he would create in United Copper as great a success as his more powerful enemies had created in Amalgamated Copper. He attempted a market movement in United Copper of truly huge proportions. He was led to believe that his enemies were heavily short of the stock and, through his brokers, attempted to squeeze them. He ignored the warnings that he was fighting the greatest aggregation of money in Wall Street.

It was pointed out to him that with his puny $12,000,000, he could scarcely hope to worst those whose millions ran into hundreds, but Heinze hoped to repeat in Wall Street what he had done in the Butte courts. He bought United Copper steadily until he believed that he had cornered his opponents and incidentally the stock.

Then came the day of settlement. He called for delivery, expecting there would be a general scramble and a settlement price which would augment his fortune. But instead, there came the stock. His brokers literally deluged him with securities, until the firm of Otto C. Heinze was forced to suspend and the stock that could not be delivered was thrown into the Curb Market, resulting in one of the most spectacular breaks in the history of that institution.

Apart from the fact that it precipitated a panic which closed banks and trust companies, it was practically the end of Heinze. His great fortune, won through years of litigation, of turmoil, of hard fighting, of bitter conflict, that brought out every ounce of courage within this genius, was swept away in a few days. Heinze was then only 38 years old.

There is not much more to the story. For a few years afterward, Heinze remained an operator in the markets, chiefly in Ohio Copper and Stewart Mining. His aggressive activities in these issues brought him a new following, but it was impossible for him through these companies to regain his position. His defeat left him more or less discredited in certain circles. And the remaining years of his life were devoted chiefly to activity in the smaller priced issues in which he was interested.

A venture in Porcupine brought him once more to the public eye, but it was practically still-born. Heinze's career, spectacular as it was, inglorious as was its end, brought great profits to many of his followers. Heinze was as vigorous in his market operations as he was in his litigation. The splendor of his buying is still remembered on the New York Curb Market.

But there is a time to fight and a time to run. And Heinze's vanity, his intoxication with his self-esteem, which beclouded his vision, at the time when he needed the greatest keenness of perception, is but one of the many tales of the near-great that have come down through the ages since Belshazzar.

ALLAN A. RYAN

*Already he has made his mark in the Street. The wheel
of fortune has made one complete revolution for him.
Worthy son of a worthy father, his first success was
carved alone and single handed. He is the exception
that proves the rule that stock market operators do not
run to a second generation.*

ALLAN A. RYAN

Once in every so often, one of the many financial writers will mourn that there is no second generation of stock market operators. The fascination of the daily combat in the Wall Street arena rarely passes from father to son. Perhaps the fathers themselves have something to do with it. The man who has followed the sea swears that his son shall never be a sailor. The doctor's aspirations are that his son shall be a merchant, and the merchant tries to tempt his son into becoming a professional man.

In the Street there have been bankers whose fathers were bankers, witness the succeeding generations of the Morgans. There have been financiers who have followed financiers, as in the case of the Belmonts. Railroad and empire builders have had sons ready to carry on their work when the burden became too heavy, such as the Goulds, the Hills, and the Vanderbilts.

The fascination of the Wall Street arena rarely passes from father to son.

But the battling giants of the market seem to stand alone. Keene, Cammack, White, Sage – they all have been isolated figures in the financial world. There is, however, one outstanding exception – the Ryans. As this is written, both father and son have made their mark in the Street. The unique feature, however, is that they have worked independently. Allan Ryan is not standing on the shoulders of his distinguished father, Thomas F. Ryan. The younger man has been carving out his own fortune, without the aid of either his father's great wealth or his tremendous experience.

The wheel of fortune has made a complete revolution for Allan Ryan, but be it said to his credit that, whether building for himself a gigantic fortune or whether, with his back to the wall, defending his possessions, he never asked for help. At various times in his market career, the name of his father has been connected with his operations, but so far as the records show, the elder Ryan has always maintained a strictly neutral attitude toward his son's operations in the market. The only thing that Thomas F. Ryan contributed to Allan Ryan's success was the younger man's seat on the Exchange, but the interests of the two men in the market have never conflicted. They have never operated in the same groups of securities.

It must be admitted, however, that Allan Ryan inherited much of that Celtic fighting spirit that was the key to his father's success, a factor that was very much in evidence in the sensational market in Stutz Motors, which brought Allan Ryan to the first page of the public press of the world.

Allan Ryan's operations in the market have been of a different caliber than those of his father. The elder Ryan's machinations

He has never been associated with operations on the bear side of the market.

were conducted more or less in secrecy. He shunned the glare of publicity. The younger man's operations, however, have been conducted very much in the open. He has believed in taking the public into his confidence and enlisting their assistance (as have many very successful market operators), of allying himself distinctly on the constructive side of the big market operations, and letting the world know what he was doing.

Apart from the Stutz episode, there might be mentioned such instances as Stromberg Carburetor, Replogle Steel, Ryan Petroleum, and many others, which have been among the more active of the industrial division of the market and in which the trading public has profited by the vigorous construction of Allan Ryan.

Ryan is a builder, a creator of values. In his brief career (for Mr Ryan is only in his early 40s) he has taken many struggling corporations and developed them into successful units of the country's business structure. As he constructs businesses, so he constructs markets. He has never been associated with professional operations on the bear side of the market. It seems to be against the very nature of the man. His dominating thought is to build, to create, to make two dollars grow where one grew before, and in that growth to foster and develop appreciation in market value, in which not only he, but the public, shall share.

No better understanding of Allan Ryan's philosophy is to be obtained than in his own words of two years ago:

"Production – buying it and developing it – that is my enthusiasm. Think of the demand! This country brings $15,000,000,000 of new wealth out of the ground every year and that's all got to be turned to human uses by production. It is the one genuine 'sure thing' there is. You can't miss on it if you follow sound business principles."

"What are those business principles?" he was asked.

"Well," he said, "the first is, don't be a spendthrift with your surplus earnings. Keep your dividends down and pour the surplus back into the business, as Mr Harriman poured them back into his railroads, until your plant is in condition to meet your demand and your financial foundation is absolutely sure.

"Another big point," he said, "is proper organization. In fact, I believe that organization is 75% of the battle. And with organization goes supervision. Every plant manager of every one of our properties has to send me every day a statement which shows the sales for that day, the production for that day, the cash in bank and various other items. In that way, everything is put to my eyes every moment. If there is any improvement whatever, we can find out at once what or who caused it and if there is any falling off, we can stop the leak with the minimum of wastage. Of course," he added, "all that means work. But if a man is not willing to work and does not like to work, he'd better stay out of business, instead of getting put out by the workers. There is no such thing as easy success and get-rich-quick ideas, in my experience, never turn out to be anything but ideas. Make yourself be patient, wait the results, is another fundamental business principle. Treat everybody square is another, whether it is your workmen, your partners, your managers, or your stockholders.

"Buy production, build it up, remember you live in America and go ahead, regardless of all fools who sell real values on passing flurries. As old Mr Morgan said, any man who is a bear on the United States is something which can't be repeated. This country is a whole lot bigger than any man or all of the men in it. Its resources are boundless. As I said, $15,000,000,000 of new wealth comes out of its soil every year. And if out of all its production, we would have sense enough to set aside 10% for surplus, if every year for twenty years you and I and every other American would set aside 10c of every dollar that comes into his income, let it compound at 6% interest, at the end of that period, there would be more wealth in America than has been created here from the day Columbus landed, to this moment."

Allan Ryan was born in New York in 1879. He received his early education at Stonyhurst, England, later graduating from Georgetown University. Through his father's connection with the market, he drifted into Wall Street, and was, in his youth, well acquainted with the elder Morgan, John D. Rockefeller, and E. H. Harriman, for whom he executed orders. His father gave him a seat on the Exchange. He broke into public notice on his own account some ten years ago, when he took two small struggling typewriter concerns, and welded them into a substantial organization.

From then on his name began to be associated with many enterprises. He was an indefatigable worker. Ryan in a concern meant the infusion of boundless energy. One after another, he took hold of enterprises that were on the sick list, and breathed into them the life of business prosperity.

He was no "son of a rich man." Many of these sons have lent their names to directorates, and about all they contribute to the success of a corporation is the pocketing of a gold piece for attendance. But Ryan was a director who directed. He was a member of the executive committee of many corporations. He might have had a life of leisure and ease, but he preferred work.

Then came the Stutz incident. Ryan was judged as having created a "corner".

He has a capacity for labor that Wall Street may well shoot at as a mark. He loves a fast car, as indicated by his once being stopped in New Jersey for burning up the highways with an 80-horsepower machine. He is keenly interested in aviation, and was once president of the Aero Club of America. He is tall and looks very much like his noted father.

Fortune rewarded his energies, and at one time, after a particularly good day, in which his securities had appreciated in value, he was worth some $30,000,000.

Then came the Stutz incident. Ryan had developed Stutz from practically nothing into a big going concern. It was prosperous, and Ryan saw the reflection of that prosperity in the rising market for the shares. It is not within the province of the writer to dwell upon the merits of either side of the controversy. Let us hear both sides:

Ryan claims that while visiting Indianapolis, he was stricken with influenza and the professional short interests attempted to raid Stutz. He said he did not create the situation. Relative to the company, he said, "I believe in the property, for I built the company. I do not care for the profits of fluctuations. It does not matter to me if the stock is $5 a share or $5,000 a share."

The other side claims that Ryan purchased all he could of the floating supply, until more than 90% was in his hands and he was able to do what he pleased with the stock and that a free and natural market was not maintained. There is no question that Stutz, at the prices to which it soared, was highly inflated. And Ryan was judged as having created a "corner."*

Ryan was expelled from the Stock Exchange and the wheel of fortune began to revolve on the down side. It ended with bankruptcy and a shrinkage in his assets from $30,000,000 to $16!

The governing board of the New York Stock Exchange is a body of wise men. However gory the battle that takes place in the

The Street is still full of stories of that memorable rise of Stutz from around $60 to $700 a share.

great arena, their position is one of strict neutrality. But against corners and manipulation of a character in which the investing and trading public may be hurt and despoiled, they are as adamant, and swift punishment follows the infraction of the rules.

Whether Allan Ryan was motivated by ambition, or by a burning revenge on those who had attempted to destroy that which he had created, is immaterial. He had broken the rules and the discipline meted out to him was no more than he might have expected, or would probably have himself sentenced an offender, had he been numbered among that just governing body.

The Street is still full of stories of that memorable rise of Stutz from around $60 to $700 a share.

Editor's note:
* There have been famous "corners" in grains and other commodities, but when it comes to stocks and shares, the "Stutz Corner" left a hard-to-beat impact on speculative stock markets in its time and in the history books also.

There is a story of the man who, getting a call to come to Atlantic City, returned as fast as a racing car could bring him, bought 500 shares of the stock and sold out later at a 100 point advance.

There is the story of the young man, who, scenting something of the sort, purchased a call for 100 shares of the stock at $130 and saw it run into an $18,000 profit before he cashed in.

There is the classic of a small trader, who, during the early part of the year, had purchased 25 shares of the stock and sold ten of them with a small loss, under the impression that he had purchased only ten. A day or so before trading stopped, he received a telephone query from his broker, asking what he wanted to do with the 15 shares of Stutz he owned. It took some minutes to revive him, so the story goes.

Is Ryan through? The Street does not think so. For some time he has been down at the bottom of the wheel, but he is still an active figure in many corporations. His companies are thriving. He is already a dramatic hero in Wall Street. He is bold, fearless, independent. He is an aggressive market operator. He is a fighter. He is a market-maker. Moreover, he has a strong following, and the street's opinion is that Allan Ryan is gathering his forces together for even bigger things than he has done. He has at least learned one lesson – that one is not privileged to carry a fight too far. Perhaps, with this tempering influence, he may yet be rated as great a constructionist as his father.

INDEX